THE
JOURNEY
OF
FALSE
PERCEPTIONS

By
ROBERT JENKINS

COPYRIGHT

No part of this book may be reproduced, or stored in a retrieval system, or transmitted in any form or by any means, electronic, mechanical, photocopying, recording or otherwise, without the express written permission of the publisher. Bible quotes used in this book are from the King James version.

Text Copyright © 2018 by Robert Jenkins

Printed in the United States of America

ISBN 978-1-945491-14-6
All rights reserved.

Published by 2 Tigers LLC

Cover design by 2 Tigers LLC

The First Edition

R – remember your commitment is first to God
O – out of your belly is healing for the nation
B – be true first to yourself
E – everlasting life is your greatest desire
R – rely only on God
T – truth, the only freedom on Earth

J – Jesus is the Savior of the world
E – embracing all from God
N – never quit
K – knowledge of the Creator
I – I am who God says I am
N – never alone
S – servant of the Most High

THE JOURNEY

From pain to purpose.

From doubt to deliverance.

And from fear to faith.

These are the reasons why truth became my search and friend.

My journey consists of many things, people, and books that have changed my life. I pray and believe that from this book and the guiding of the Holy Ghost, that you will be brought to the light of your purpose and passions as well.

ACKNOWLEDGMENTS

I first will acknowledge my father Robert Jenkins whom I love and thank God for my mother, the late Pat Brown, who was the embodiment of truth from both sides of life.

To my only brother, Todd Jenkins, who was and is the rock in my life, the one who has remained true to every moment, whether good or bad. Thanks Todd you are my hero.

Last but not least I would like to thank my wife, Cassandra Jenkins, who is my best friend and the strength that brought me to the light in a very real way. I love you always and always.

SPREADING THE TABLE OF CONTENTS

		The Opening	09
Chapter	1	Genesis	13
Chapter	2	The Needed Talk	15
Chapter	3	Passing Down the Pain	18
Chapter	4	A Painful Identity	23
Chapter	5	Truth Turned Inside Out	32
Chapter	6	The Power of Being in a Place of Power	47
Chapter	7	Question Time	58
Chapter	8	All Laws Must Be Examined	60
Chapter	9	The House	62
Chapter	10	Dreams	79
Chapter	11	Commitment	81
Chapter	12	Fighting to Be	83
Chapter	13	Having a Date with Death	84
Chapter	14	When Love is a Problem	87
Chapter	15	Finding the Truth is More	101
Chapter	16	Cracked Vessels - Fixed or Filled?	113
Chapter	17	Thoughts from The New Landlord	121
Chapter	18	I Am Afraid	125
Chapter	19	Recovery	137
Chapter	20	The Picture of Your Life	139
Chapter	21	The Result of a Disconnection	143
Chapter	22	We Were Made for Life and Love	157
Chapter	23	Let Us Pass Over unto The Other Side	160

Chapter	24	Known in the Flesh, Overlooked in the Spirit	167
Chapter	25	God Hears You Too	177
Chapter	26	Being Center, Being True, and Being Real	180
Chapter	27	Add it All Up	182
Chapter	28	Nakedness is the Dress for Glory	184
Chapter	29	Honesty Will Cause You to See God	186
Chapter	30	Healing the Family from the Beginning	190
Chapter	31	Living a Life of Legacy	193
Chapter	32	Joy and Pain During the Journey	195
Chapter	33	Identities Stolen	199
Chapter	34	Nevertheless, Not My Will	226
Chapter	35	Freedom by Death or Freedom by Truth and Life	228
Chapter	36	The Powers of Words	237
Chapter	37	Victories	258
Chapter	38	The Law of Faith is The Law of Release	261
Chapter	39	God's Purpose and Our Problems	269
		About the Author	271

This page is intentionally blank.

THE OPENING

Day One

If you don't know why you were born, why you're here, and you question the purpose of your life then don't put this book down.

As you read my words, you may begin to think that I am crazy. So did I, but I'm learning everything was for those 'crazy' thoughts. I didn't know I'd have to walk out the book before I could write it.

There were many voices in my mind and my pain was great but then I heard God say, "next", and I stepped out of the line called Victim.

Day Two

Sometimes being called 'crazy' is only the road to being understood. When I was much younger, my friends and I would see someone playing basketball really well or playing the drums, and we would say, "man he is crazy on those drums!"

What we were saying was that he was outside the limit that we had put in our minds. You are not mad (as being insane), but your passions and purpose can't be defined by the box of yesterday.

Day Three

Never allow the mistakes of man to be the reason for quitting anything in life. Remember that God uses the foolish things to confound the wise. Only God can have a plan that includes mistakes by man and it still comes out perfect.

Day Four

- Pain has a way of taking you back to your past.
- Pain looks for agreement even if things agreed are not true.
- Pain will lie to you about yesterday just to make today's pain seem so real.

I allowed the absence of my father not being in my childhood to dictate who I was not. I was mad because my father was not what *I thought* he should be in my life. I judged him without a jury or facts. I wanted to believe that because he had not been in my life, I would not be loved, or have any worth. When pain is felt, it will tell you to get a chair in your mind and then it takes some circumstances - past, present, or future - and places those circumstance in that chair to support your feelings.

From then on, you/it use/s this place to justify your next actions. These become lifelong reasons never to allow anyone to hurt you again, which becomes your first line of defense. This is the first establishment of your reality, not God's Truth.

I did this for years, and this kind of thinking made me question myself.

Most of my life I questioned who I was, or what I was. This became my conviction, which told me that no one would be there for me. Who could identify me or with me? Over the years I thought that I was only an accident of pleasure, not a person of purpose. You can see from reading these things that I believed my conception was not under love but force and pain. I was acting as if God had left me in the hands of a man without a plan or purpose for my life. I lived under these mindsets for years, which put me on a search for pleasure when what I needed was to know God's Purpose for my life.

If you make yourself a victim without purpose saying, "this was a part of God's Plan," then these 'truths' will take you down, not up and that can't be a purpose from God concerning your life.

When people tell you that your beginning is terrible, it makes you ask, "why continue on the journey?"

Day Five

I must learn from it all; surely there has to be a good reason why I suffered so much? It is questions like this that will put you on the right road where you begin seeking God for the right answers.

Day Six

So I learn, fight, and see. Then I cry, move, and begin to walk out of the false perceptions into the truth concerning my life.

Day Seven

Truth has come, and I am happy for the first time, based on truth and not lies. So I breathe, smile, and then I say okay what's next?

CHAPTER 1

Genesis

When you are young and pregnant, influences can come from everywhere - family members, pastors, schoolteachers, but in my case, it was from my grandparents. My grandfather was a preacher; he was the preacher that preached holiness or hell. He believed that watching TV, women wearing pants, and going bowling were a sin. People called him Papa Jenkins, a very strict man who lived by those Old Biblical Principles. My grandfather was well known in the city and had great respect within our community.

My grandparents did not **get married for love. For them, love was not required, but obligation was**. My father's real mother hemorrhaged and bled to death right in front of him. He watched her die because, at those times, in the early 1940s, many black families could not afford to call an ambulance. When my father's mother began hemorrhaging they attempted to help her, but there was nothing that they could do; they lost her while she lay in my grandfather's arms. This left my father, his two older sisters and his father alone. Well, my grandfather heard about a woman who lived in Mississippi whose husband had died and left her with one daughter also. Being moved by her problem of raising a daughter by herself and him raising his children alone, my grandfather decided to write her a letter. She was so moved by it that she agreed to marry him, deciding together they would raise the children. They never had children of their own. Because of this, they believed that sometimes a relationship **is about obligation and not always love.**

In my mind, I believe that one of the main reasons why my father and I did not connect was because I felt not only did he not want the obligation of me being his son but he did not love me, at first. I believed that my mother just happened to get pregnant. **Law moved him not love in my book. And I hated this and anyone that I thought did not love me out of "love." To me, love that is ruled by force is forced-love, and I see it as equal to rape. This kind of thinking grew branches in my mind, and yes, it did bear much fruit.**

Sometimes, how you start is how you will end, if there is no truth being revealed while on the journey.

CHAPTER 2

The Needed Talk

My father and I went a long time without a journey, without those talks that lead to truth. Even though I was born his son, he became my enemy. Every day those emotions of hate that I had for myself, because of how I saw myself and how I thought he saw me, became greater.

It became an undercurrent of pain, shame, hate, and anger to the point that it blinded every truth about me. I would wonder why my father didn't love me; if there was something wrong with me. I'd question if he really was my dad. I heard stories about him having other children besides my brother and I. **Finally**, at the age of 35, my father and I had our first real talk. It was all about why he wasn't in my life and why he didn't try to raise me.

I had been waiting for years to talk to him about this. I had so many questions and was filled with so much anger. See, even after my father and mother got divorced, my father, by working in the mill, made good money. He had a great house, was able to drive brand new cars and dated fine white women. I hated the fact that I had never spent a night over at my father's house. I was not allowed to call him until after 6 pm because his girlfriends, whoever they were at that time, would say he was "taking a nap." They were told not to wake him even if it were his sons calling.

I hated how, one time, my brother and I wanted to go to the movies and we had no money. So, we called our father, and instead of him giving us money, he brought over his penny bank and said, "count the pennies" then to call him and tell him how much it was. I was so hurt because to me he was saying, "my sons are only worth my left overs." But we counted up the pennies anyway and went to the movies. While there we heard a voice that sounded like our father. I looked back; there was my father behind us with his white girlfriend and *her kids*. My brother and I were so heartbroken that we just got up and left.

I said to myself, "he has time for some other women's kids, knowing he has two sons of his own." Here I am looking like his twin, and I can't even spend time with my dad. I could not wait to talk to him about how he had two sons that were raised by a gay guy and not one time did he talk to us about the danger of this or not one time did he ask us if there was anything going on. I just wanted to hear him say, "be a man and don't let no man have sex with you," or hear him say "if he touches you, call me I will kill him." I was looking for my protection, and it was not there. I was mad about that.

The time to talk had come, and his words to me were,

"Veil, (which was my nickname, as I looked him in his eyes with tears and great concern) my dreams were to play the guitar all over the world and be famous. **I didn't know how to be a father and didn't want to be one.** Do you think that I wanted to work in a steel mill like my dad?" he said with tears in his eyes.

"Veil, I was a good-looking man and could play that guitar well. Everybody loved me. I had girls and a great future in front of me. I was a young man, and then your mother comes and tells me that I'm a father and that wreck' my whole world. Veil, you know that my father was a very hard and religious man. He never hugged me or told me that he loved me.

Our life was centered around church, all day on Sunday, Tuesday night Bible Study, Friday night services, and Y.P.W.W. **(this stands for Young People Willing Workers)** and about 4 revivals a year and 3 shut-ins, (that's when you stay in church all day and all night and sometimes with the door shut and locked). You know that no sports was permitted because, to my father, that was a sin. I'm sorry son, but I didn't know what a father looked like, I only knew rules, and that's what made me leave my father and run away.

So what could I show or tell you? I thought my music would free me from my father and the pain of my own childhood. When you were born, I felt trapped and I ran. I didn't want to be a father, who I didn't know how to be anyway, **and I was not going to act like I did. Yes, I was self-centered, and I only thought about me."** And then he said, **"I love you and please forgive me, but I only did what I knew how to do at that time. Son, that was where I was, and I made a big mistake."**

CHAPTER 3

Passing Down the Pain

Well, after that talk and many other events in my life, I came to understand things a lot better. I begin to understand this concept called generational curses. I am not sure if I want to blame the choices that I made on my father, but I will say that mindsets or voices from your past, or voices from those along your path will visit you and hope that you receive them as your parents did. If your father is a drinker and his father was a drinker, then you may end up being a drinker too. Not because you are cursed to drink but because the same reason that made them drink and the mindsets that they used to cope with these kinds of problems may be the thought pattern in the family.

I now believe more that thought patterns are passed down through a family line rather than curses. When you carry your father's blood, you may also carry his ways and his thoughts. Have you ever thought about why some families are full of preachers, singers, and even businesspeople? These things can be passed down through your D.N.A. and also by culture.

There is much more in the human bloodline than looks, skin color, and talent. I am saying this because after my father told me about his life with his father, this showed me the mindsets that had been and were continuing to be developed. His father married out of obligation, and my father married for the same reason. His father didn't know how to show him love and my father didn't know how to show me love either. As you read on in my story, you will see that I married, not out of obligation like my dad, but out of my need to heal my pain and also the pain of my mother.

When I was a very little boy, and people would ask me. "what do you want to be when you grow up?" I would say a "father and a husband." I was hoping, even as a little boy, that if I would be a father and a husband then, maybe, I could heal my pain of not having a father and also the pain that I saw my mother go through from not having a husband. This pain in my life was so real to me that I tried to be the savior for my mother and myself. As a young boy, I decided to be the man in the house and said to myself I would protect my mother.

When my mother would have men come over to see her, I would run down the stairs real fast and open up the door, then shake their hands real hard as if to say, yes there is a man in the house. I was experiencing the same mindsets as my grandfather and father. Most of my life I married women that needed help in some ways or another because I thought that saving them was healing my mother's pain and mine. Also, that if I help them, for sure, they would love me.

Do you see the mindset here, how my grandparents thought that marriage could heal their pain (now don't get me wrong, this was a great leap of faith that my grandparents took, and it worked for them)? They stayed married until they both died even though, many times, my grandmother questioned if papa loved her, and then there were times that she knew he did. But back then, love was expressed in different ways than now. Still, the point here is that my father thought marriage could heal my mother's pain and his parent's beliefs.

All the time the mindsets of how to deal with pain were being passed down and never questioned. See, many times it's not the things that we do because of circumstances, but it's the things that we are not willing to talk about in the midst of our choices. **Sometimes, we think we have to choose between two lesser evils, (and this may be true), but we should always talk to someone about the choices that we are about to make.**

Don't hide the pain by not talking about it or the choices even when they must be made. When you don't know if it's the right choice to make, still have conversations about it.

"This is not an excuse but a reality – you are born with seeds of positives and negatives, which ones will you choose to water?"

In the Bible in Acts Chapter 3, it says a certain man lame from his mother's womb was carried. This means that he was wounded in the womb. There are many of us who were wounded from the womb, even before we could speak or hear anything;

there was a seed of bondage waiting for time to reveal itself to us. Apostle Paul says in:

Ephesians 2:2-3

2. Wherein in time past ye walked according to the course of this world, according to the prince of the power of the air, the spirit that now works in the children of disobedience:

3. Among whom also we all had our conversation in times past in the lusts of our flesh, fulfilling the desires of the flesh and of the mind; and were by nature the children of wrath, even as others.

We were born with blessing and bondages, but most of us are open for the blessing but lie or try to ignore the bondages.

Remember that oppression and repression are real even if you deal with them or not. The only difference between the man in Acts Chapter 3 and I was, not only was I wounded in the womb, but I was also being carried by the pain, fear, and disbelief of my *perception* of love. I allowed my environment to nurture the negative instead of learning what to do with negative seeds. All things have a purpose and a reason, even our so-called falls and failures. I want to share with you some very powerful but alarming things that I was told to show you; how mindsets are placed to establish a hold on your life.

Now, just think if your mother took a hanger and placed it in her womb while being pregnant and attempted to kill you. And yes, that did happen to me. I believe at that time I felt her shame and guilt of being a church girl and having a baby while not married. I believe I felt her feeling of letting her family down, loss of respect among her friends, and disappointment in herself. Especially losing her dream of going to school to be a nurse, because that was so important to my mother.

My mother lost blood, but I believe I lost hope as well as identity. Still, I did not die. On top of all that, when she went to church, she would roll on the floor acting like she was in the spirit, but she was actually trying to kill me, yet I lived. **When she finally went to the doctor to see if I was ok, they said, "Pat he is alive, and we don't know why, but he is."**

Can you imagine all the emotion that was going on in my mother's mind while carrying me? **These emotions should have been my awakening of purpose, but instead, it became a delusion of my pain. It became the beginning of my search for love, and also my journey of learning. As I look back, I can now say, "all those lessons were necessary for the awakening of purpose and passion."**

CHAPTER 4

A Painful Identity

The main reasons why we may question our ability is, sometimes, we think that we are out of place and this brings feelings of not being wanted. When something is healthy and placed in the right position, it will function properly, like a fish that is placed in water automatically begins to swim. But if it has been wounded, then it will not do what is natural. Being wounded always makes you question your place of purpose. It's a dangerous thing when we believe that we are in the wrong place without knowing where God wants us to be. These mindsets make us rush into things and can cause us to move from the place that will prepare us for our future. Because where you are *is* where God wants you to be so as to learn the lessons for the *next* place.

Life lessons must be taught *by* life! To believe that you are a mistake or in the wrong place is to say that God lost you somewhere. For I have learned that every lesson in life must cultivate the acknowledgment of who you are. Each lesson is trying to tell you something, so listen. Every one of us should become conscious of God's Purpose and presence that lives from within. This presence is always talking, but there is also the noise that comes from pain trying its best to control the conversation, hoping that you will respond to its confusion.

Pain speaks very loudly, and its best friend is 'fear' who is the 'bondage keeper'. Fear will name you and then protect the name it gives you. If you try to rescue yourself from that name, your pain and his friend fear will fight you as if you are their enemy. You will be surprised at how pain and fear will have you protect and defend a place of hiding while at the same time this hiding place is killing you and your purpose. Pain and fear don't want to be removed, so they set up walls to hide behind. Most people will identify with their pains and fears before they identify with their purpose. We should never allow our experiences to name or define us, only God.

Remember that the voices of pain and fear are clear and they have justified reasons to name you. Pain and fear will say to you things like, "the rape was real, very unfair; you have a right to be angry and bitter." The divorce was real, so pain and fear say, "never trust again." Pain and fear take pictures of the people that hurt you and paste them on your eyelids and from that point on you see through those eyes. From then on, whenever you are looking at people, you are really looking at the same pain that hurt you. By pain and fear alone, you can become a victim of life.

Let's talk about Leah in the Bible:

Genesis 29:31-32

31. **And when the Lord saw that Leah was hated, He opened her womb: but Rachel was barren.**

³². And Leah conceived and bared a son, and she called his name Reuben: for she said, surely the Lord hath looked upon my affliction; now, therefore, my husband will love me.

It was pain that named the baby. You would be surprised at how many things we give birth to out of pain and fear.

Genesis 29:33-35

³³. And she conceived again, and bare a son; and said, Because the Lord hath heard I was hated, he hath therefore given me this son also: and she called his name Simeon.

³⁴. And she conceived again, and bare a son; and said, Now this time will my husband be joined unto me, because I have born him three sons: therefore was his name called Levi.

³⁵. And she conceived again, and bare a son: and she said, Now will I praise the Lord: therefore she called his name Judah; and left bearing.

Her first pain wanted her to be looked at; the second wanted her to be heard; the third pain wanted her to be attached, held. Finally, when she let go of her pain and fears she was able to praise God. All of this was from the pain of rejection, fear of loss, and being hated. Her pain named the children, and how many of us were named by our parent's pain, rejection, and fears?

Pain, The Blinder
We only have a love problem because we have a God problem.

For years I ignored and sometimes just closed my eyes to the emotional pain that I was carrying. I had to learn that there was a difference between being blind and just sitting in a dark room. Being blind means that I am not able to see but sitting in a dark room just means that I rather act blind, or just didn't want to put the lights on. These are the kinds of lies that we tell ourselves, because in our mind the truth about us doesn't fit our birthplace. There were times that I would find myself saying things like, "my mother never had the chance to experience love, so I will most likely end up like her and never experience love as well." My father is alone today without a mate, and I hear voices saying to me, "YOU ARE NO GREATER THAN YOUR FATHER!" This is how pain keeps us comfortable. Pain shows you the natural side of things and uses those things as a measuring tool to bring negative mindsets. This so you can go no farther than the ones that hurt you.

Pain will always hinder your advancement if you let it. I think about the Prophet Elijah who was a great prophet of God but when Jezebel wanted his life, the Scripture says in:

1 Kings 19:4

⁴· But he himself went a day's journey into the wilderness, and came and sat down under a juniper tree: and he requested for himself that he might die; and said, It is enough; now, O LORD, take away my life; for I am not better than my fathers.

These were words from a man that saw God work and was a witness to God performing miracles in his life, but he was still haunted by his past and his father's failure. He compared his life to his father's and believed that if his father only went so far, then how he could not go beyond that point. Pain will always have you compare yourself to your failures or something that will cause you to feel like you are a failure. Pain will also lie to us and make the very people that tried to show us love, share God's Word with us, and God's Strength become our enemies. Pain will cause you to turn on your friends and see them as enemies. Pain places a voice and a belief deep inside of us that asks, "how can they love you, when you don't love yourself? How can they have for you what your father did not?"

Brokenness causes you to reject love, and it will push people away that try to love and deal with you. This pain will make you create ways to get rid of them. It will show you things that are not really there just to support the belief of you being alone now and always. These voices will cause you to be praying to the God of life to bring death to your doorstep. I was this person for years, preaching life and wishing for death. My greatest sermons were right before my greatest pains.

I would walk the streets and hope that a car would hit me. I would wish that a sickness come over me so I could leave this world that refused to love me. I would say a thing like, "everyone wants my gift but who wants me, who loves me for me?" Words like, "the only reasons why I have friends is because I can play music and preach." I was a walking dead person. And the real pain was when I realized that all 'my truth' was *my perception.* It was *all* lies to keep me wanting and looking for something on the outside that I had always inwardly possessed.

The best way for pain not to be discovered is to look at others' faults and blame them, while you, on the inside, are crying for help. Pain is a jealous "friend" that wants all of your attention. And will fight for first place in your life. This is why pain tells you that others cannot be trusted; that others are liars - all so that, at the end of the day, you and pain can say, "it's true, it's just us!" Pain becomes the blinder to the truth about life.

 ## Pain, the Keeper of Past Thoughts

We, as people, love to blame everything on the devil rather than give God credit even for the negative. Now don't get me wrong because there is a mindset which is influenced by the devil or the devil's system. But that system needs a human mind to be activated in.

Let's look at 2 Corinthians 10:4-6. This chapter is about spiritual warfare but did you notice that the devil is not mentioned, but your thoughts are?

2 Corinthians 10:4-6

4. (For the weapons of our warfare are not carnal, but mighty through God to the pulling down of strong holds;)

5. Casting down imaginations, and every high thing that exalteth itself against the knowledge of God, and bringing into captivity every thought to the obedience of Christ;

6. And having in a readiness to revenge all disobedience, when your obedience is fulfilled.

If I am going to be truthful about my struggles, then I must be truthful about my thoughts. Honestly, I was trapped between two opinions; because I wanted to hide what I thought of myself behind preaching and playing music. Still, on the other end, blame everyone for the pain that I said *they* gave me. This made me live a double life: happy in public but very sad in private. If you met me in my bad times, you might never know it, because I loved to laugh and act crazy but most of the time that's when I was saddest. My smile was the hiding place for my pain, and if I could make you laugh, then I would feel like my life was not so bad because somebody likes me. Here is a question, "are you sad and saved?"

It was revealed to me that anything less than the design stops the fruitfulness of it and I was not designed to think of myself that way. How can I feel like, "I'm the greatest car in the world but no one wants to drive me?" If that car had a soul, it would be depressed while shining. It took a lot of pulling down thoughts, dreams and the strongholds of beliefs to learn that painful journeys will teach you that God has approved every event and experience in your life - all sent by God to place you in an environment of power even when you feel weak.

You may have been the one who made the decision, but you were not the one who designed the plan. These lessons are designed to teach you how to see and hear the purpose and plan of God for your life: the real you, the one that God created will be revealed through it. After all you're seeking and searching for you will come to find out that you can be no greater than whom you are right now, but the secret is that you must know *you* and love *you*. Spiritual growth is the understanding of yourself and your experiences. Knowing yourself makes it possible to stand for *you*. Not until this happens should you enter into an intimate relationship and be healthy.

This was a very hard lesson for me to learn and it took me years to understand that my heritage is too great and my life is too important ever to be compromised. If you have this kind of thinking, then this is what I suggest, turn the truth in and let the lie out. Basically, as Morpheus said to Neo in the movie *The Matrix*,

"You have to let it all go, Neo. Fear, doubt and disbelief...then jump and remember everybody falls the first time, but at least you are falling as a freeman and not as a slave to your perception."

CHAPTER 5

Truth Turned Inside Out

In my mind, God's Truth about my life was not the truth that I believed, at first. It took years for me to separate the difference between my reality and God's Truth. In our reality, we can allow things and circumstances to not only name us but also give us a name that defines us. We believe that the name which was given to us identifies *who we are*, not knowing that this is just *where we are* at that time. In other words, just as names are given to identify a person, names can also locate a place or a mindset. Again, names can be given to locate the places where we are at, and do not necessarily mean that is actually who we are.

Other times names are given by how we behave or what people see in us at that time. I have to repeat this, the names that are given to us are not necessarily who we are. Still, this is how I reacted to my circumstances, and once these experiences named me, I also began to act out according to the labels I put on myself and believed in. Just like Jacob in the Bible and how his family gave him that name (which means 'trickster'), he began to act out his name, and so do we. But God changed his name to 'Israel', which means 'one that strives with God'.

It takes years for us to believe in our God purposed name and not the name that perception and pain may give us. Your perception is your reality, but God's Truth about us is what we really should believe.

Philippians 4:8-9 reads:

8. Finally, brethren, whatsoever things are true, whatsoever things are honest, whatsoever things are just, whatsoever things are pure, whatsoever things are lovely, whatsoever things are of good report; if there be any virtue, and if there be any praise, think on these things.

9. Those things, which ye have both learned, and received, and heard, and seen in me, do: and the God of peace shall be with you.

Now, these are some strong words, because when you say, "whatsoever is true, honest, just, pure, lovely, and good report," these seem like perceptions, not truths. What may be true to me may not be true to you. **We have a habit of making what's true, honest, just, pure, lovely, and good report to God not the same for us because of our own perceptions.**

Our perceptions of our birth, life, and death are most of the time not the view that God sees. Was it true that my mother and father really didn't love me, or was their love not perfected to the place where I desired it to be? How can I say who loves, when I don't know what love looks like? Are we honest when we cry for something? Or are we just like a baby that uses crying as a way to get what they want and not what they need? This is why The Word says **"think on these things"** *and please before you conclude something, give your perception a lot of thought before you believe that it is God's Truth.*

Are we loving or scheming in the name of love by acting in a way that tries to bring people under our control? **True love sets you free to be you; it doesn't control you to be what others want you to be.** These are the kind of questions that we must ask ourselves to see if we have not turned the truth inside out to meet our own needs. The truth can be hiding behind a word as well as in a name; this is why, in the Bible, God sometimes would change the person's name so that they could see who they really were and not what life and circumstances had told them they were.

Many times, because of our environment, the truth is turned inside out.

Jacob, in the Bible, was never meant to be the 'trickster', but life has a way of robbing us of who we are, by allowing us to define ourselves based on what we do or by what we have been called. Jacob was his given name from birth. Why would you give a child a name which could form him into the very thing that was not his design? If you name me before I discover who I really am, how much work do I need to do to free myself from that name?

The more you hear something, the more you may start to believe it. This is why calling people names and especially without knowing the truth about them, can hurt the person's insight of themselves.

Have you ever thought about the people who are called 'gay' as a child and many years later still can't get that lie off of them? How many things name us, before the DIVINE SIDE is revealed in us? By that time our parents, life, and circumstances have already named us, which now confuses us about our purpose and passion. The problem with words is that they also carry a spirit, so even when a word's spoken over you, it's the spirit of that word which may oppress you. Once it finds agreement (you believing its definition) it then gets inside your mind, convincing you that what they say is true. The power behind words can turn the truth inside out if you don't know its power or don't know how to fight the *spirit* of a thing verses the thing itself.

I grew up with people who had names like Killer, Smoke, and Slick. These names were associated with some of their behavior and mindsets. But the truth is before they were born, God had a purpose and plan for their lives, which did not line up with the names they were being called. Most of them ended up living out the man-made-given name and not their God-given purpose. Some of them just say, "it takes too much work to become the real me, after being the wrong me for so long." Others say, "this is the only me I know, and *this me* is loved, adored, and gets respect so why change?"

One person told me that when he walked in a room as himself, no one moved or even spoke to him. Yet, when he came out of jail, with the name Killer, and walked into a room, everyone began to move and speak. "So why would I give up that name and respect that I received?" he continued. This is a great example of the truth being turned inside out. It's bad when you rather try to kill who you were born to be and keep alive the lie about yourself because of outside forces and delusions.

One of the main reasons why we do this is because of the fear of truth, "What if I am not what I think I am?" Or the fear of loss because "if I accept the truth who will stay with me?" These are the main reasons why people lie because most of the time, telling the truth comes with a loss and cost. When I was young, telling the truth got you a beating so we lied in order to take gym class the next day; or sometimes telling the truth could get you killed. One of the greatest fears is the fear of failure because who is really ready to accept failure as a truth? And often, if I'm honest, I don't even want failure to be a stepping-stone.

We really fear the greatness that is in us because this brings on reasonability. Within each of us is an inner urge to live life to its fullest but we ignore or try to crush this urge because of these fears. We want to share that fullness with others in the world, but life and circumstances often rob us like a thief in the night, especially when we think that we're never wanted or accepted. If you allow it to, fear will create a profile that gives a negative mindset about yourself.

I have learned that negative self-thinking caused by pain causes us to renounce potential. This kind of thinking causes you to search for achievement and accomplishment from the outside, instead of finding wholeness and fulfillment from within. I was so delusional about myself; I believed that I was born unwanted; I didn't ever think that my problems could have been in the divine plan of God. Just because this may have been what I was born into, should not mean that's the way I had to live or die.

I have many friends who chase away impactful people in their lives, because of fear that hides behind their intelligence or in their "hardness." They find themselves alone again, but the reason is because of the fear that's fighting in ways which run these people off. These fears can become judgmental just to make people say, "you are too judgmental," and leave. Pain then tells us that negative things are bad; the bad thing making us think we **are bad people.** Such thinking is so far from the truth. You will never be able to bring the truth about you out if you don't begin to think on these things repeatedly, checking to see if they are true or if it is just your perception at that time. Just because your beginning seemed to be negative does not mean your life cannot become a positive picture in the end. **Spend time with your Creator; the one that made you, for the only person that should label the clay is the potter.**

Truth, the Reflection Light

Do you remember long ago, before these new cameras came out, that when you took a picture, you would make sure you were under some light? But the development of those pictures had to be done in a place called the dark room. These undeveloped pictures are called negatives, which become 'positive' pictures later on. Well, in the mind of God, the picture of your destiny was taken in the light. But the negatives must be developed in the dark places, and those dark places are called 'the dreadful things that happen to us, by us, and sometimes through us'. These things may cause us to have low self-esteem, fear, rejection, pain, and unforgiveness. But it's only by God doing the developing that He will produce a wonderful picture of your life.

Let's reflect back over Joseph's life in Genesis 37 when it says;

Genesis 37:18-24

[18]. And they saw him afar off, even before he came near unto them, they conspired against him to slay him.

[19]. And they said one to another, Behold, this dreamer cometh.

[20]. Come now therefore, and let us slay him, and cast him into some pit, and we will say, Some evil beast hath devoured him: and we shall see what will become of his dreams.

^{21.} And Reuben heard it, and he delivered him out of their hands; and said, Let us not kill him.

^{22.} And Reuben said unto them, Shed no blood, but cast him into this pit that is in the wilderness, and lay no hand upon him; that he might rid him out of their hands, to deliver him to his father again.

^{23.} And it came to pass, when Joseph was come unto his brethren, that they stripped Joseph out of his coat, his coat of many colours that was on him;

^{24.} And they took him, and cast him into a pit: and the pit was empty, there was no water in it.

All of this was his dark place, to develop his character. It was in God's Plan; as hard and cruel as it was, this was also necessary. Sometimes the most negative pictures come from family, friends, and church people. Later, God brought Joseph from the pit to a prison and then he finally ended up in the palace, (which was a blessed place) and it put him in a position of authority. He, now, had character and position so when his brothers and father were in hard times, needing his help, he was able to forgive and bless them. One of the ways to know when the truth is in its rightful place is when you can forgive and help those who have so-called hurt you.

Well, the point of the story is that, without knowing the light, a negative mindset not only tells you that you are bad but also that you are unloved, rejected, not understood, in the wrong place, or born into the wrong family. Without foresight, this can cripple your passion. This thinking causes you to second guess your very nature. If your mind or your thinking is in the wrong place, then so are you, at that time. If you want to change how you see yourself, don't look out at people or things around you but change how you're thinking. We were created in the image and likeness of God, and all things start in the thoughts of our mind; your mind will create their environment.

If you think you are not loved, then the perception from your mind will create an un-lovable environment. Your mind will furnish the environment, just like God furnished the world with trees, the moon, the sun, and the stars. So what is the furniture of an unloved place? It is pain, rejection, being misunderstood, and the greatest of them, *"no one loves me"* conversations that you will have with yourself and others.

Forsaking Truth, Convinced by the Lie

To defend your false perception, you will begin to build images as a fence of security. These images can hide in religion, politics, and personal needs. Sometimes you don't even know that you have built these fences. They have become invisible protection in the name of religion, politics, and relationships.

These images also manifest as symbols, ideas, and beliefs. You will be surprised by how we will defend our symbols, ideas, and beliefs even if they keep us in bondage. Question: Does a wedding ring say she is faithful? Or does carrying a Bible say, you know God? See the burden of these images dominates man's thinking - in his relationships and daily life. These images can be the causes of our problems, for they divide man *from* man. One's perception of life is shaped by the concepts already established in their mind. Man's consciousness can control his entire existence. "Am I the color of my skin," or "is my color no different than the paint on my house?"

I know that sounded crazy, but these are just some of the questions that we must begin to ask ourselves to locate these images. This is why one of the first questions that God asked man was, "who told you that you were naked?" And unless we begin to question what we think and why, we'll begin to believe we're what we think. If anyone tries to change your thinking, it makes you perceive that they are trying to change you. This is when your fence of security goes up, protecting you. The images used in defense will be of religion and anything that will help keep them alive.

When truth initially comes it will, at first, feel like you are being attacked. This emotion is common to all humanity, saved or not. Man's individuality can be destroyed by a false name. His form and the superficial culture he acquires from tradition and environment can shape him. The uniqueness of man does not lie in the superficial but within complete freedom from the false consciousness; again I say this is common to all mankind.

One of the great strengths of these false images is their ability to make us feel comfortable, secure, and religious. These things tell us that we are good and kind, feeding upon self-gratification. We must fight to not be convinced of the lies that feel so good. This is a very hard thing to first admit and then to bring under correction. One of the first signs of growth and freedom is when you admit to these false images that you have built and are willing to destroy them. There are questions that we all need to ask ourselves in order to locate these images. Questions like, "where does my security lie?" "Who told me the things that I believe the most and why do I really believe them?"

Proverbs 3.5-7

5. Trust in the Lord with all your heart; and lean not unto your own understanding.

6. In all thy ways acknowledge him, and he shall direct thy paths.

7. Be not wise in your own eyes: fear the Lord, and depart from evil.

Here is a Bible verse that tells us to lean not on our own understanding but acknowledge God concerning the matter and then allow His ways to direct us. But in:

Proverbs 4: 6-7 it says

6. Forsake her not, and she shall preserve thee: love her, and she shall keep thee.

7. Wisdom is the principal thing; therefore get wisdom: and with all thy getting get understanding.

In one verse it looks like our understanding should not be trusted but in another verse it looks like God wants us to get understanding with all that we have. I believe that the revelation is that we cannot comprehend without God and sometimes we will not understand even Him, which is a reality that we should come to grasp. In other words, question God and the Holy Spirit about everything that you *think* you know and get an understanding that you may, at that time, fully comprehend.

Because We Lie

God had been placing His trust in me all the time, even while I was so mad at Him about my life, my mother for marrying a man who struggled with homosexuality, and for me having a father who didn't know how to be one. But God was saying, "I put you in their trouble to help them, not to curse you. Yes, I put you around sexual problems because I also gave you power and authority over sexual problems." God revealed to me that most of the time our purpose is also our problems.

I learned from my own problems how to be honest and anointed. You are listening to a man that indulged in sexual sins on Saturday, and on Sunday morning got up and went to church to preach wondering, "why and how could God still use me?" This was confusing, but it woke me up to my call and my problems, while teaching me not to lie since God knew about them and still decided to call me. Sometimes we are like Peter who had a revelation of Christ through his spirit but lied in his flesh. Or like Abraham that believed God would give him a son when his wife was barren but lied about his wife when she could have been raped. Abraham could trust God for providing a son, but not trust Him for protecting the one that the son would come through. And the reason for all of this is so that when other people look at you and think that we're losing our minds, we can say, "no!!" These problems come with being anointed.

Here is a great example of what I am saying; Show me a worshiper, and I will show you a person who is also highly sexual. Because worship is intimacy from the spiritual side, but the flesh wants the same experience from the natural side. So when your spirit is done, your flesh says, "my turn." These principles are true in many regards. Like, if you show me a prostitute, I will show you discernment. A prostitute learns how to discern their clients. She or he must discern which ones are crazy, have money, and which ones are freaky. Did you know that most people who tell jokes and make others laugh are sad themselves?

What I am trying to tell you is that the person who has the answer is also carrying the problem. When Apostle Paul, was Saul, he was an enemy against God but in this same man was two thirds of the New Testament. We all need deliverance, but needing deliverance means that we are all in this dark fight for light, and in our deliverance we are facing and fleeing! Most of us would rather flee, hide, blame and lie than to face deliverance and be honest, one of the greatest troubles in our lives is that people really can't handle the truth. So we lie and keep ourselves in bondage.

The truth is that we lie on God as much as we lie on the devil. We are in situations that look like God never started, never co-signed. Let's learn just to tell the truth that *we do lie*. We don't want to believe that God is in some things that hurt us or He brings a struggle to us, so we lie. We knew that some things that we were in would not work, but we wanted Him again to save us, to rescue us in or from something that He never wanted. *Maybe* it was never in His will; or was it His will to use all things for His glory?

Here's the truth. We were lonely, broke, desired sex and could not, or would not, wait. We had children without a father, bills without money, a body without a man, low self esteem without a cheerleader. We were like Jezebel without an Ahab, or maybe this is you - lived so bad, slept with so many, that with the next one, you said, "I am going to do it right. I am going to get me a saved girl/guy, a pure girl/guy." Disregarding your lustful desires, love for money, love for power, and now all you have is a 'saved girl/guy.' Or maybe this is you - got a good husband that goes to work, (wow!) comes home from work, loves the kids, but no romance, no flowers, and you are not being appreciated. He's just a good workhorse. Guys, flip that around to fit the description of your wife as needed.

Question: Is this God's Fault, or was it your choice? Did He allow you to have some trouble which brought you to a place where you can still be used even with all these kinds of troubles? Are you willing to be honest about your troubles or are you still hiding and blaming? Could it be that all things work by the will of God?

CHAPTER 6

The Power of Being in a Place of Power

A seed needs a place called the ground, that's its place. A bird needs the air, that's its place. The fish need water, that's their place. So, where is your place in life? Adam was created in the image and likeness of God, but he still needed a place of purpose. The garden was his *put* place. The put place is where God *puts* you to do your purpose. But Adam let sin remove him from his put place. Remember all sin starts in the mind. God never creates anything without giving it a place!

There was a man in the Bible whose name was Moses. One day, walking in the desert, he saw a burning bush that was not being consumed by the fire. This perplexed Moses so when he went to the top of the mountain where the bush was, God spoke to him from the burning bush. He told Moses to take off his shoes for the place where he stood was holy ground. The ground was not holy but, *the place* was. There is a spiritual place within the natural place in which we all stand. The question is not what you think or believe but it's *where* those beliefs and thought patterns are standing in and sometimes standing on.

It's not only what you see, but also what you are looking through. If looking through a green lens, then what you look at will have a green reflection. The place where Moses was standing had everything to do with how he was thinking about himself.

God's Presence will always reveal your true thoughts and this is really how you find yourself; how you become real by being in a place of truth.

Here is a man who was born in the time when all male children of Israel were being killed; the king, at that time, feared the strength and might of these Hebrew people. He decreed a death sentence over the Hebrew women that "at childbirth, if the baby was a boy, kill it." Death was looking for Moses at birth. This sounds like my life. Death will come to the place where you are called to bring life and try to bring death to that place and you. If you can't overcome death, then how can you do your assignment and bring life?

Every great man of God has to overcome death at the beginning of his life. Look at Cain and how he had to face death, by his brother, right at the beginning of his life; Moses, Jesus, Joseph, you, and me. Just think back and see that our fight started before we even got here. It was your struggle from the rip that should have indicated to you how much your life is a threat to the enemy's kingdom. It's essential for us to overcome our enemy in order to help others overcome their enemy. Because of the presence of death, pain, and fear it may look like you are out of place.

Let's look at the life of Moses (which is really our life too) and see how death tries to take us out and confuses us about our place. So Moses' mother put him in a basket to hide him from Pharaoh's decree, but the water took him to the Pharaoh's daughter. Sometimes, life takes us to and through the very places that we think we should run from. God will allow the water of life to drive you to your place called *journey*. We are driven to places that bring us to our destinations of identity and maturity. These places are necessary and God knows what's best for us even when it hurts.

If the truth be told, sometimes we would have never done the things we did or be in the places we were just because we loved or obeyed God. No, the truth is we have to be driven. Moses was driven right to Pharaoh's daughter and when she saw him, she loved him, deciding to raise him as her own.

Now let's look at this and remember that Moses was still a Hebrew boy and should have been killed but was yet alive. The killer of the Hebrew babies was now the one that would raise him, not only that, but in the same house where death was. Then the daughter of the enemy put him back into the hands of his real mother. The one who wanted to kill him, the one who feared the strength of his growth is now raising him as his own. Sometimes it's in the plan of God to have your enemy raise you. Can you believe that you are in the right place when being raised by the ones that want to kill you, or the people who rape and hate you? These are great questions but remember, only the dark places can reveal what was really taken by God. Give time 'time' to develop the positive pictures in your life.

These places are uncomfortable, painful but are only for a time, to prepare and develop the greatness, purpose, and passions that are in us. As we read on, this same king trained Moses, and because of who his father was, it gave Moses an opportunity to be educated, respected, and to gain character.

Now let's look at how God's Perfect plan was already in effect: Hebrews were not educated but because Moses was being raised as the king's son, he was able to learn how to read and write, which was in God's Purpose, because, later on, God would use him to write the first five books of the Bible and also write about his life story. The message to be told is that, in God, it's never the wrong place or wrong things; there are always lessons being learned to give help in the future. These are hard lessons but the presence of our purpose must be felt, realized, and acknowledged in our spirit before the potential *in* us can pour out its power.

Suffering will bring the gold to the surface. After experiencing it you will know that you have touched a divine power but you cannot explain to another just what it is. This is because you have gone beyond the actuality of your words and have made union with *the cause side* of existence. It is the quickening of your divinity, through the power of the Word, that brings us to this place. The divine nature, that is in us all, is waiting to be brought into expression through our recognition of the power and might of God in us. Suffering will bring you to a place of power.

It's Not the Wrong Place

Moses' mother had to make a choice to either to let him die or let him go. There are times in your life when you **take a temporary loss for a permanent gain.** One of the hardest lessons for me to learn was how to let go of the things that I believed I needed - like love, family, and being married. The voids in my life became the prisons of it. If Moses' mother had not let him go, then he would have been killed. Can you let it go and trust God or do you hold on to it and suffer it to be destroyed? Think about this when you are in a hard place and don't know what to do. Believe it or not the things that we are not willing to let go of will kill us or enslave us to the need of it. And with this need, we will never be fulfilled. All the sex, money, and fame will never fulfill you. You and I were created by God and for God; only He can bring happiness, completion, and fulfillment. Imagine that God himself takes his Hand, places it in the ground of cement and when that cement becomes hard, the only Hand that will match the cement perfectly is His. Well, that's your life and only the life He has for you will fulfill yours perfectly.

There is a prayer in the Bible that Jesus taught and part of it says, "Thy kingdom come, thy will be done on Earth as it is in Heaven." God's Kingdom cannot come until your kingdom goes, so let it go and trust God! Apostle Paul says in:

Philippians 3:13

^{13.} Brethren, I count not myself to have apprehended: but this one thing I do, forgetting those things which are behind, and reaching forth unto those things which are before,

A greater meaning for the word 'forgetting' is 'letting go.' If you don't let it go then you may never move on. Moses' thoughts of being raised as a king's son and not as a slave had to be a challenging place in his mind; he had to have questioned himself and his purpose. Was it luck that the mid wife ignored the king's decree and kept him alive? Was his mother putting him in a basket which ended up in the arms of the king's daughter luck? Is this the reason why I am here or was it God's Purpose all the time? These are some of our questions as well. Like, was it really by accident that I was born, can sex really make a baby or is this a gift from God by the means of sex? Was I chosen or cursed? The truth is that Moses was in the right place at the right time. While it seemed to be a bad place, it was where he needed to be in order to get to where he was designed to go. Sometimes you can't get to what you are not willing to go through.

There is another Bible verse that says,

Romans 8:28

²⁸· and we know that all things work together for good to them that love God, to them who are the called according to his purpose.

If "all things work together for good", then don't leave out *all* things. Later when Moses' time was up living under Pharaoh, he killed a man because he could not take seeing his people being oppressed, and he ran, but guess what? The place he ran to was, again, the right place. Sometimes, it takes a form of death to show us that our 'time is up' and to move to the *next place*. You know this by the grace of God and when the grace has moved so should you. Again, even in your running, hiding, and other things, this will be a dark place to bring you back to the light of the picture that God saw from the beginning. Moses running from a problem took him to the answer where he saw the burning bush and heard God say, "the place where you stand is Holy ground." You can learn here by knowing a purpose in one place will take you to another.

The word Holy means 'to be set apart.' God was saying, "the place where you are now was set apart for *this cause*." Every experience is a set apart place so you can hear His voice and learn from that place. Take off the shoes; why the shoes? Because they carry thoughts from the last place. You needed them at that place, for that time, but now you are somewhere else. Once the thoughts bring you to your new destination, exchange them for the thoughts of *that place*. Jesus told His disciples that he would go to prepare *a place* for them. This was after He said, "in my father's house there are many mansions, but the place has to be prepared." **The real place is *you*;** every day and in everything, *you* are being prepared.

We are all walking through the mansions in God's House, which are really rooms, or the eyes of GOD. If we keep walking, we will see the place called *you*. Don't turn this truth inside out, and don't curse this place just because you are not in control or don't understand.

In **Ephesians 4:22-27** its says,

22. That ye put off concerning the former conversation the old man, which is corrupt according to the deceitful lusts;

23. And be renewed in the spirit of your mind;

24. And that ye put on the new man, which after God is created in righteousness and true holiness.

25. Wherefore putting away lying, speaks every man truth with his neighbor: for we are members one of another.

26. Be ye angry, and sin not: let not the sun go down upon your wrath:

27. Neither gives place to the devil.

The place of doubt is God's Place to reveal faith. The place of worry is God's Place to reveal trust. And the place of confusion is God's Place to bring peace. In other words, don't let your thoughts of the flesh take place in your mind; this is giving place to the devil. We were made for God, and being in the right spiritual place, even in your mind, is very important. If the house is clean but no one is living in the place, dark thoughts, (demons) will visit that place and begin to live there.

A Place for Your Seeds (Thoughts)

A good seed needs dirt to grow. Did you hear that? I said *dirt*! These are your secrets, and your regrets. The dirt in people's lives that gave them revelation of God's Love and forgiveness will surprise you. Did you know that when a seed is put in the ground that the dirt attacks the seed to bring death to that seed? The seed needed the attack in order to release the tree. In others words, I am saying that God will cause your circumstances to bring death to your way of thinking so that His potential and power can be revealed through you. What you and I think are accidents and failures are really training classes for purpose. It's our dirt attacking our seed; it's our problems and secrets that are trying to release the revelation of God that was in us all the time.

John 12:24

24. **Verily, verily, I say unto you, except a corn of wheat fall into the ground and die, it abides alone: but if it dies, it will bring forth much fruit.**

You must be alone in death, and later, be accompanied by fruit. Knowing that you are in the right place is very important to your freedom and thinking. But most of the time being in the right place also brings death and loneliness. You can't bring fruit, if you are not willing to, first, be alone. Do you think, that the little fish that are in the sea or the big fish that are in the ocean are saying, "can I do this?" Do they question their ability to swim or does the water become one with their purpose? Could it be that the air makes it possible for the birds to fly and the ground waits for the seed to be planted? It's funny to me, when I think about nature, and how no one taught the birds to fly or the fish to swim or even dogs to bark. Because it's in their D.N.A. If we were created in the image and likeness of God, then what's in our spiritual D.N.A. to the point that we will not need to be taught? We seem to need people to teach us, which could be the problem, especially when the lessons are against our very nature.

The true voice from within must be heard above any outside source. Pain can reveal purpose but should not make us a victim of our past, which becomes our future problem. Looking back on all of this, I can see when my thinking was being attacked since the day I was born, and my purpose was also being revealed from that day too. The seed of my purpose was looking for the dirt of my destiny to be planted and begin to grow. In the word "planted" is the word "plan," **it's God's Plan that is plan-ted.**

CHAPTER 7

Question Time

What does God think about you? This is one of those questions that, if it is really understood and received, would free you from the power of rejection, fear, and the need to be needed. The answer to this question is also the substance to any emptiness in your life. But the question must first be asked, because how we think is the door that leads us to either our real or false self. The problem that stands at the threshold of triumph is misconceived thought. Everyone becomes pregnant with a seed of thought. But *whose* seed is it? Both faith and fear comes by hearing.

Therefore, you must always examine *who* is speaking into you and also which one of you is listening. The flesh and the spirit are listening at all times. Question is, which one's prepared and ready to respond to what they just heard? I am learning how to not allow anything or anyone to be god in my life besides God himself. But if these thoughts are not from God then I have allowed another law in my mind to be god and have believed that it is God himself. This, when the reality is they are my thoughts which I believed at that time. This is why all thoughts must be examined under the light of truth.

You may say, "how can we know when it's God and when it's not?" Well, again, all revelation comes by questions. Our truth must be based on the thoughts in the mind of God then we will learn the laws that demonstrate how God thinks. Remember that the laws of the universe, like the laws of music and mathematics, know only how to *be*. Everything about God is always in perfect being. So here is another question, can you just *be*? How do you define yourself when you are doing nothing?

CHAPTER 8

All Laws Must Be Examined

The law of God is love and, love is the fulfillment of the law. Jesus came not to destroy the law but to fulfill it. But it was God who so loved the world that He sent Jesus. Then this means that Jesus is a by-product of God's Love or we can say God's Law? Such is one of the most important truths to learn, the law of love. It's seen to be confusing even in context because how can love be a law. Galatians 5:22 talks about the fruit of the Spirit; that there is no law. But this is not saying that the fruit of the Spirit are not under a law, more like there is no law that can hold them.

Now, this is a great thing to know because it will reveal to you about the strength of the Spirit and about what's in us that cannot be lost. There are other laws in our members (of our body) that will try to overcome the law of love. I have come to learn that the real problems are those laws that try to bring us into captivity to the law of the flesh. This thief has been trying to rob you from the beginning of your life by making you believe that your circumstances have cursed you. However, the truth is that all of your problems were just opportunity to BRING THE REAL YOU FORTH. And the real you is not looking for love; he/she is love.

I have learned that all that I was going through, God had allowed it so that He could build His house, and if I am His house then that's where He lives. Yes, I am saying that God lives in us.

From the day that you were born He was building a place for Him to dwell in, and you are that place. All of this is really about God.

CHAPTER 9

The House

We must have a revelation of any place, person, and purpose that God has put us into. But the greatest revelation is of self because God already knows who He is. The main reason why GOD will reveal Himself is so that He can also reveal you to *you*. Jesus asked the disciples, "who do you think I am?" and then Simon Peter said, "you are the Christ." Then Jesus said to him, "flesh and blood did not and cannot reveal me but only my Father which is in Heaven." But then He said, "and you are Peter, and upon this revelation, I will build my church." We know the church is not a building but a called out people. In others words, it is through questions that bring us to the revelation of God and also to the revelation of ourselves, that we can start building the structure of self.

Psalms 127:1

[1.] Except the Lord build the house, they labor in vain that build it: except the Lord keep the city, the watchman walks but in vain.

There must be a realization that we are inadequate on our own to build anything on truth unless we have truth, first, in us. God is not building a house of brick and mortar but rather a house of flesh and blood. Flesh and blood cannot reveal God, but God will reveal Himself to flesh and blood.

Ephesians 1:9

9. Having made known unto us the mystery of his will, according to his good pleasure which he hath purposed in himself:

Philippians 2:13

13. For it is God which worked in you both to will and to do of his good pleasure

Philippians 4:4

4. Rejoices in the Lord always: and again I say, rejoice. It's a hard saying but all of it was in his will and his good pleasure.

When we can get pleasure out of pain, it is also the time when we see purpose out of problems. One sign of a growing economy is the increase of building projects, and the same is true of the divine economy, but we must let God do the building. In God's House called you, do you talk from the position and not from the practice? Let's look at some scriptures and see if we can get some help from them about this.

Romans 7:23, Apostle Paul is talking about how he saw something within himself. In his own words, he says,

23. But I see another law in my members, warring against the law of my mind, and bringing me into captivity to the law of sin which is in my members.

The great thing here is that Apostle Paul was able to see some things. The first insight was that there was another law in his members (of his body). Regardless of how saved you may be, there will always be another law, in you, fighting against you. Before you begin to fight, first learn to be honest about what's *in* you. Now, this law is very smart because it will have you fighting others on the outside while the real problem is on the inside.

Abraham had two sons, Ishmael and Isaac. One was a son of the flesh, and one was a son of promise, but don't forget that they were *both* Abraham's sons. Adam and Eve had two sons, Abel and Cain and the Bible says that Cain was of the wicked one, but they both were sons of Adam's family. We all must be honest about what's in us, and about the things that come out of us and from us. Unless we are ready to admit to the problem and where the problem lives, then we will never be able to solve it.

The next thing that I see here is that this other law, in my members, is warring against my mind. Now we must remember that the physical flesh does not have a mind, but there is a mind of the flesh. In other words, there are some things that I just want - God calls them "the lust of the flesh" and they are thoughts that are still in my mind. But there are also other thoughts from the Lord that come from my spirit. These two thoughts are in a battle, but the fleshly thoughts are bringing me into captivity. Wow!

Now, this is real talk. It means that my flesh, based upon what I want, will put me in prison, which also means that I am locking myself up in prison because of what I really want. This is what I was doing, and you have been doing this also, if you're honest. Our flesh and desires become the policeman, and our own mind becomes the prisoner. We lock up and lock down our selves but then, from that prison that is made by us, we holler out to the world, "it's your fault!" We blame our father, mother, and friends for what we did to ourselves because it's all in the mind of the individual.

Another insight should be this other member; the one that can bring your mind into captivity. This tells me that it has some strength and to not to take it lightly. If it is strong within itself, then how strong will it be if I don't fight it or try to ignore it?

Last but not least is that my own thoughts take me to the law of sin, which is very dangerous because if I am a prisoner to a law of sin when I should be a prisoner to the law of the Spirit, my behavior is reflecting my war from within. This kind of war will have you living a sinner's life as a saint. What do you do when you are a saint with a sin problem? This is one of the greatest wars from within, and this kind of battle can kill your witness and your light especially to people who are not honest about their wars. We have to fight from the sinner position until we win and learn to be lead by the Spirit through practice. When I am in this place, I have learned to tell my mind that I am free indeed. Only by this confession can I begin to set myself free. The reason why I say *set myself free* is because, truthfully, I was already free in Christ, but by my own lust, I allowed myself to be drawn away. So now, it must be by my own will and confession that I set myself free. If we are not honest, then we will never be able to say where we are. And if we can't say where we are, then we are stuck right there, in that lost place, fighting something that we refuse to accept.

Romans 7:25

25. I thank God through Jesus Christ our Lord. So then with the mind I serve the law of God; but with the flesh the law of sin.

    This verse does not say that the law of the flesh was being removed, but Apostle Paul does say that he would serve, with his mind, the Law of God. The same space that is in your mind for the mind of the flesh is the same space that is there for your *renewed* mind in Christ. The question is *who* will occupy that space? Who will you serve, your old mindset or your new mindset? We must learn how to be honest about what is in us and who is leading us before we can answer this question. Remember this,

Romans 8:5-13

5. For they that are after the flesh do mind the things of the flesh; but they that are after the Spirit the things of the Spirit.

6. For to be carnally minded is death; but to be spiritually minded is life and peace.

7. Because the carnal mind is enmity against God: for it is not subject to the law of God, neither indeed can be.

8. So then they that are in the flesh cannot please God.

9. But ye are not in the flesh, but in the Spirit, if so be that the Spirit of God dwell in you. Now if any men have not the Spirit of Christ, he is none of his.

10. And if Christ be in you, the body is dead because of sin; but the Spirit is life because of righteousness.

Philippians 2:5

5. Let this mind be in you, which was also in Christ Jesus:

When you look at all the things that you have gone through, ask yourself what mindset did this put you in? Do you have the mind of Christ concerning them or a mindset from the pain of them?

Hebrews 8:10

¹⁰· for this is the covenant that I will make with the house of Israel after those days, said the Lord; I will put my laws into their mind, and write them in their hearts: and I will be to them a God, and they shall be to me a people:

¹¹· And they shall not teach every man his neighbor, and every man his brother, saying, Know the Lord: for all shall know me, from the least to the greatest.

Genesis 12:1

¹· Now the Lord had said unto Abram, Get thee out of thy country, and from thy kindred, and from thy father's house, unto a land that I will show thee:

It is very hard to be what God has called us to be, when we hold on to the mindsets of our environment. Here, God tells Abram to leave his country, his people, and his father's house. These are mindsets that can control the thinking of a person and may limit how much of God's Assignment and understanding that they will receive. I remember the first time I quit my job by following the Holy Spirit, how many of my family members began to say that I was lazy and didn't want to work. Or the first time that I decided to go to college and my family said that I thought that I was better than them because some of the people in my family did not go back to school. These are mindsets that can hold a person back.

Romans 12:2

2. And be not conformed to this world: but be ye transformed by the renewing of your mind, that ye may prove what is that good, and acceptable, and perfect, will of God.

How do you think of yourself now and what are the thoughts in your mind? You must ask these kinds of questions on a daily basis. Remember that old mindsets are like gravity; they are designed to bring you down. This is why Jesus said, "if I were lifted up from the earth then I would draw all men unto me." The mind of Christ must be lifted up from the earth realm first and then the drawing begins. How you view yourself may be based upon your perception. When you strip yourself of things that you have given permission to define you, then how do you now see yourself and is it based upon a Christ mindset? Also, the things that you speak out of your mouth are signs of the things that live in your mind (house).

There were many times that I would find myself saying, "I will never be happy," or "no one loves me," or "people just don't want the truth." But I did not know that these things were so much alive in my mind. You should talk only about the things that you want to see live and grow. You must understand the power that is in your words, and if you believe this then do you take responsibility for your words? If whatever you speak out of your mouth would begin to live and grow, then how much of it would help or hurt you?

Your thoughts should be the previews of the coming attraction and if you don't like what's coming then change what you're thinking about. Your words are the announcement of your future, so ask yourself, how much do you lie? The truth is that God's Thoughts are words but God's Words are pictures so when you tell what you heard Him speak it tells me what you saw. There will come times when we realize that words should bring vision to the earth realm. But before this happens, every thought of personal possession must be dropped out of the mind before men can come into the realization of the invisible supply (God's Mind). A man's mind may be likened to a garden, which may be intelligently cultivated or allowed to run wild. This is why we must learn the laws of thoughts. It's not what you do in public but what you think about when you're all alone. When we alter the way we think, we lend ourselves to God's Healing law and miracles occur.

Every event and experience in your life has been approved by God, if not set by Him, to place you in an environment of power. You may have been the one who made the decision, but you were not the one who designed the plan. The lesson is designed to teach you how to see and hear the purpose and plan of

God for your life. You must always keep, in the front of your mind, that *your spirit* knows your destiny. What you are seeking and searching for has always been with you. Then you must decide to explore, accept and understand how to make it work for and with you, always remembering that spiritual growth is the understanding of yourself and your experiences.

Is your identity developed? Is it developed from the spirit or the flesh? Is it developed from what people saw and named you or what God saw and named you? One of the benefits of this is knowing that you make it possible to stand up for yourself, in an intimate relationship, without taking over the other or losing yourself to the other. This lesson cost me to lose myself just like the prodigal son. I lost my house and many others things, but after the class was over, I came out knowing and loving me. Not only will that happen but also developing God-confidence gives you the ability to handle a relationship. I had to come to an understanding that self-worth comes from God's Appraisal, not mine. We must be willing to pay the cost to know and be who God says that we are. This lesson may also cause you to put down what you feel you are to be led by; what you believe.

The Foundation of the House

I have learned that, most of the time, feelings only tell you where you are, not where you *should* be. Feelings, however, have thoughts as their foundation. Emotion can bring you to a place of healing, but if there is no inner conviction to sustain that emotion, the healing is not likely to be permanent. I believe in the power of agreement as stated in Matthew 18:19 referring to if two agree. The revelation is about thinking and feeling. Our feelings tell us where we are and what we believe. If they agree, God will be in the midst of them to give direction. Most people are either not honest about their feelings or not honest about their beliefs, which hinders the true building of the house. If the foundation is built wrong, then the house is in danger of not handling the pressures of life. All foundations are in our thoughts.

Now that we have asked some questions about the foundation, let's move to another room in the house (another question).

The Living Room of the House

The living room are the thoughts that give us life. This is the room where we really live. Are you living or having life? Many people have a living room but how often do they live there? Many people exist but how many people are really living? You can't live beyond your thoughts, nor can you grow. So if you don't like how you're living, check how you are thinking. Don't ever forget that your heritage is too great and your life is too important to ever be compromised.

If you compromised God's Thoughts for you then this is the beginning of you experiencing the fall which is the coming short of God's Glory (the spiritual bank of being and knowing all things). Most people have a TV set in their living room. This is the box that controls programs that we see. It's called the television; telling us about man's vision, it can create our perception of people, places, and things. The thoughts from this room will bring us to a place of comfort and also a place of delusion, if we are not careful.

What do you watch the most in your living room? As I said before TV stands for television. What visions do you tell yourself? Are they set in this room? Can you be challenged or is your mind made up by what others have said, by what others have believed? Is this a room of comfort, and how comfortable are you? Or are you struggling with something in your spirit that says there is more? The thoughts in your mind, can they rest or are they sleeping? Well, don't abandon this room because you can never have life where there is no vision. But always check where the vision comes from and why it is needed.

Vision is birthed from wholeness and not the need to be whole. It's hard to have vision where there is no peace. Peace comes from *the being*, not *the doing*. Remember that peace is an indicator that Christ is on broad, and whenever a vision is given, the enemy will come to destroy that peace. But if you can be still in the storm, the storm will cease. Thoughts of God will bring you or keep you in wholeness, which is really what being born again, being perfect, and Holy is all about. Okay, let's move to the next room (thoughts).

The Dining Room

This is the room where we eat, and most of the time where we eat in an intimate setting. Who eats with you (in your mind)? Are you still eating with your mother's eyes and how she saw your father? Are you still eating with your father's attributes and how he treated women?

Jesus said to eat His Body and drink His Blood. And unless you do this, then you are not able to see the Kingdom which is where the thoughts of GOD ARE. What do you talk about and who do you talk to (in your mind)? How often do you make love to thoughts that give birth to the devil's children (thoughts of darkness)? This room is very personal and can be very dangerous because it is where we allow guests (thoughts of others) to dine with us. Even though this is not the bedroom, a lot of spiritual intercourse goes on here.

The Kitchen

This is where cooking is done. Also, it is the place where undeveloped thoughts wait to be birthed. The ingredients of what you eat. Can you taste the ingredients in the food or thoughts? Well, it's like this - when the Bible says to taste and see that the Lord is good, this also implies that tasting the food will open up your eyes and show you the goodness of God, because the goodness of God is what you have just tasted. We have been eating food that was prepared with doubt, fear, and pain but we were so hungry for love that we swallowed it fast, missing what it truly tastes like, just to say that someone fed us so they must care. Yet, later in life, we became sick and unhealthy, blaming the cooks and the cooking, and at the same time becoming accustomed and having an appetite for this kind of food. It's not only what you eat but also *who* has prepared it. "Adam, who told you that you were naked?" One of the greatest understandings in the Word of God, to me, is the understanding of what is in disobedience. It is that, from one man's fall, all became sinners and that Nature knows all things both from the sides of dark and light.

Bathroom

This is where waste is released and the body is cleansed. This place is a very important room in the mind, because it can reveal who you are and are not. It is where truth is the mirror, and it will not lie regardless of your station, position, and even your title; it only shows you the truth. This mirror is really the Word of God at the place where you stand. The mirror can reveal to you your ways and your dirt but it does not play a part in the cleaning, only the revealing. Cleaning is when you are honest about what you just saw and are willing to face it in order to flee from it.

The bathroom, also, is the place where you empty out what is no longer needed in the body. If you hold on to the things that are no longer needed you bring sickness to the body! Most new homes have closets in the bathroom as well, so this means that sometimes, there are thoughts within thoughts that need to be examined in this room as well.

Who is the Head of the House?

Is your husband (the Holy Spirit) the head of your house? Well, remember this position is always under attack because the flesh will not give up its rights without a fight. And one of the ways that it thinks it can win is by having as many visitors as it can. Note, when I am referring to a visitor, I am referring to thoughts such as fear, pain, insecurity, doubt, and the list goes on and on. The purpose for each visitor is to make themselves roommates.

When you have roommates, you also give them permission to stay in the house. They will live there rent-free! But the spirit must recognize them and, on a daily basis, begin to remove those thoughts. Many times in the Bible we read things such as "think on these things," or "let this mind be in you that was also in Christ Jesus," or "take no thoughts for tomorrow." Who lives with you can determine how you live.

Questions and Statement for the House

Do you have an unlawful roommate? (Don't be unequally yoked). Before you think that I am talking about people, remember first that I am talking about unlawful thoughts. Thoughts like, "I am nobody," and "nobody loves me." Thoughts like "I am weak," or "I am not able." These are visitors, and they must be put out! These thoughts will speak to your emotions and will confuse *loving self* with *pleasing self*. Remember that they came to the house to be intimate with you because they know that unlawful sex allows the enemy to date you; to control you.

The Bible says that if you sleep with a harlot, you become a harlot too. Now the spirit man knows the truth about you and will declare this to you if you will listen. Yet, many times, because of our needs and unwillingness to be honest, we compromise. So we entertain these thoughts and before you know it, these thoughts become actual people in our lives. There were many times that I would say to myself, "how did I get hooked up with her?" but the truth was that I was already hooked up with that thought, which manifested as her. I became the prisoner to my own thoughts in the flesh. So, now I say to you, know who you are and who you belong to first, and from that point you will stop compromising and begin to remove the visitors.

It's really simple if they are not the one, then stop spending time with them. You must, at all times, remind the flesh about the new landlord and then change the locks if the wrong person has a key (i.e. change the thoughts!). Ask yourself who has a key to your mind, and your emotions? Because the best person to live with *is you*.

I had to learn this by God striping me down to nothing and then allowing me to enjoy having nothing. Then He began to teach me how to slow down because I had been in bondage for so long all I wanted was to be free, but only to either prove that I was free or to get back in bondage again.

Relocating These Things in the House

Belief

I think that one of the greatest questions in our life is what do you believe in and why? If you can't start to believe in something, in spite of what you go through, then life will swallow you alive. Belief is the first flashlight to see what God has given you.

CHAPTER 10

Dreams

I have always dreamed to better myself. We didn't have much growing up, but this did not kill my dreams. For some reason, after all the falls I've had, I would still start over and begin to dream again. I have learned that your dreams must be bigger than your odds. But that's up to you to make it that way.

The purpose of being a dreamer is for you to see where you can be in your subconscious before you see it in reality. But remember dreams are for those that are asleep so, after you dream, you must wake up and bring what you saw into reality.

There is also a negative side to dreams, and that is when you have a dream and then create roles for that dream, expecting people to act out your dream without even loving them *for them*. See, we can pick people because they fulfill our dreams and not because we love them. Now the dream is controlling people or using them for selfish gain only. I believe that any dream that God gives you is for others and not just for you.

When God showed Joseph a dream concerning him being higher than his family, it was not to make him think that he was better or that he was greater, but it was to show him that he would be placed in a position to help his family, not abandon them.

Remember, God will always bring character to match the dream. This character is building the house.

Dreams without love become prison cells. The skill required for you to successfully live life is the "power of imagination." Without imaginations your present situation will only bind you and you will probably die in your current dilemma. However, if you learn to dream, you will free yourself from the time and the place of your present circumstance, live in your original destiny, unmarred by time and sin.

CHAPTER 11

Commitment

I was always a very committed person. If I gave you my word, then I was going to do my best to bring it about. Sometimes, you have to be committed to the commitment but remember that real commitment comes from purpose and vision, not from the need to be loved. Being committed to *truth* is the real fight. This will take focus and much prayer. Commitment, sometimes, means standing alone, especially in your beliefs and revelations. All things must be tested before they can be exposed. The test for commitment is abandonment, and you still stand. Just because you are committed doesn't mean it won't hurt and that you will not cry but you stand anyhow. How committed are you? Jesus' words say in,

Luke 14:26

26. If anyone comes to me and does not hate father and mother, wife and children, brothers and sisters-yes, even their own life-such a person cannot be my disciple.

Unless you hate mother, father, brother, and sister you cannot enter into the Kingdom. Wow, now that's commitment!

Philippians 2:5 says,

5. Let this mind be in you, which was also in Christ Jesus:

6. Who, being in the form of God, thought it not robbery to be equal with God:

7. But made himself of no reputation, and took upon him the form of a servant, and was made in the likeness of men:

8. And being found in fashion as a man, he humbled himself, and became obedient unto death, even the death of the cross.

    This is commitment at its best because this word declares that Jesus is God and He was still committed to dying on the cross. Many people are willing to be committed to greatness but not to suffering. It takes being committed to change your mind and without commitment, you may start many things, but you will not finish them.

CHAPTER 12

Fighting to Be

In order to see a change, I had to be willing to fight and not quit. Quitting is not in my blood, but winning is part of my inheritance. The strength behind it all is that if God is for you, He is more than the whole world against you. But remember again, we do not fight to *do*, but we are fighting to *be* what God has called us to be.

You can't allow your situations to define you, but your situations should cause you to question why you are here, and how you can and will get through this. There is a divine order for your life, and until that is revealed, blessings in full are withheld. Anything less than the design stops the fruitfulness of the design. Never give up the right to be, it doesn't matter how hard it gets, this is your right.

The fight to be, comes from the inside of you. You are stronger than you know, and there is a knowing in you that carries this strength. You have been called many things, but who you (be) has a name and a power from God. God is right in *all* things, and He said be fruitful, be holy. These are just some of things that be in you. So fight beyond the negative words over your life and be happy, be beautiful, be successful, because your greatest fight **is to be.**

CHAPTER 13

Having a Date with Death
(Death is Real Loud When Purpose is Silent)

When I was young, my mother had a friend that stopped believing in Christmas. So, my mother stopped believing in Christmas and I remember the first year of having no Christmas. Going back to school having nothing to talk about. Having no new toys hurt me really bad, so every year around Christmas time I would get very depressed. This one particular Christmas I was in Buffalo, New York and I was so depressed. There was no church for me to preach at, and I wasn't playing music anywhere - I wanted to die. See, when purpose is lost life becomes meaningless.

That same night I took a whole bottle of pills. I had been talking to some preacher friends outside my door and I told them that I was tired of life and wanted to die. They said to me, "please man, go on with that. Not you! All the word that you have in you?" They said this while laughing, and then they said, "you will be alright," and left. That was the first time I went through with it. I took a whole bottle of pills and went to sleep. Well, you know that I didn't die because I wrote this book some years later. The point is that pain will have you think that life is not worth the fight for purpose and every year, even now around Christmas time, death comes to my mind asking for a date.

Living with death is a very depressing thing. Wanting to die over and over again, sleeping in the bed and feeling a spirit holding you down, and having dreams of falling… this was my life for years! Fighting demons was very common for me. I remember, in my first marriage, when I was fighting a demon in my sleep and I didn't know that I was fighting in the physical as well. My wife, at the time, caught my hand just before I hit her. I would also be in church and feel a death spirit walk past me. See, for me, not having Christmas was more than "not having Christmas." My mindset was that I did not deserve to be rewarded, or I would not be loved. I would rather die than not be loved or not have someone to show me love. This fight with death, for me, was just like many people in the Bible: like Mosses and Jesus - their very births brought death to their presence.

I remember another time in my life, and it, again, was with my first wife. I was on my way to bed, and as I walked past my bathroom I saw a stronghold demon, I believe it was a stronghold demon because it looked like Mr. Clean in that commercial that was on TV. I said out loud, "I'm going to bed and I am not dealing with any demons tonight, I'm tired." I went to bed and fell asleep. While sleeping, some spirit came over me and tied me down. I could not wake or get up, not even speak. I saw myself in some realm standing in front of three demons with charcoal gray hoods on. They had no faces. It looked like a prayer line but there was only me and them. I heard them say, "if he falls, we got him," and in my mind I said, "no!" Then they touched me and I began to fall and, all of a sudden, one of my hands got loose but my body still could not move. I began to write in the air "Jesus" and as I got to the first letter "s" I heard them say, "we are losing him, we are losing him." When I got to the last letter "s" I stood straight up from the bed.

I called one of my friends who also was a preacher, and he said, "man, somebody is trying to put a spell on you! You must get those demons out your house!" I began to take my hands as if I could see those demons and throw them out my house and as I was throwing them out, my front door was shaking like something was really going out. From that, I have learned that only through facing your fears will an understanding of purpose come. This will help you see how important you are to the point that death itself tries to make a date with you.

You must yield to the Spirit of God because there are mindsets that try to rob you out of purpose. See, the truth is that just like with Job in the Bible, the devil must get permission to take you out, and God will never allow that before time. But the purpose of the devil is to get you to believe that your purpose is no good on Earth; so die. Every day of my life I must make up my mind to stand the devil up. While he is waiting on me, I will be at the dinner table with the Lord and not with the thoughts of death or even wanting to die. It's funny how, when I look back on this, it was all because I didn't get a gift from man, that I wanted to kill the gift that was given to me by God.

CHAPTER 14

When Love is a Problem

Sometimes, it seems like the people who love God the most, go through the most trouble. I believe it's because God knows the power of His love in us and can trust us with it. Take a look at 1 Corinthians 13 and how the Bible says that "love suffers all things, hopes in all things, and bears all things." Love often has a function that is beyond our character. Just like fire that has a function to burn, loves' function is to love. Fire that will burn on the grill and burn on the stove but will also burn the house down with the children in it. Because its function is to burn, it doesn't take the responsibility to think about its function. Well, love is the same way. Regardless of how bad people may be, love says, "this is how I function. I suffer all things, endure all things and have hope in all things." So love says, "when asking me to love, be ready for the function."

Have you ever seen a mother's love for her son who is on crack, or a woman who loves her husband even after he's hurt her? We say things like, "that's crazy!" or "she's a fool!" Well, is God crazy for dying for a sinful world? Is God a fool for loving a sinner like you and me or was He just showing us the strength of His love? He knows that His love will not give in and with His love, we will finish our assignment, regardless of the trouble.

Believe me, this is easier to preach than to live, but it's real and true. And yes, I hated knowing this about love because it hurts to love someone that will not or can't, at the time, love you back, yet you still love them.

You can't show me anyone that was used by God that didn't experience the trouble that comes with *love*. Matter of fact we are called and given a purpose because there is love trouble to solve. Remember that trouble is an opportunity to show the strength of love. Yes this hurts and it really pulls on your character. Sometimes, I wish God's Love could be shown in another way besides dying to self and being crucified. But being nailed to a cross seemed to be the best way to show sacrificial love, especially when you don't have to.

"The one who fears is not made perfect in love."

(1 John 4:18)

The above is a very deep verse in the Bible because if we look at Job's life, we read that God said that he was perfect and upright, but Job had a fear. When he was attacked by the devil, he said that the very things that he feared had come upon him. This is saying to me that yes he was perfect by law but not by love. Perfect love will cast out all fear. The whole story was about using the devil to perfect his love in God, and guess what, all that you and I go through is about perfecting our love for God too.

One of the main reasons why God allowed so many things to happen in our lives was to bring us to a place of honesty about where we are and who is really controlling us. Fear was controlling me even while advancing in my work place, or it would tell me don't you sing in public. This fear had me afraid to go home a different way, I mean it was crazy of all the places that fear would talk to me at. Have you notice that in almost every great leader in the Bible that God would say to them fear not, neither be afraid? How many things are stolen from you because of the fear that is silencing your mouth? I was afraid for years to talk about my struggles and even in writing this book.

My fears had me always questioning myself, like do you think you are good enough for her? There were many women that I thought would be great for me, but each time my fear said, she would never be with you! Do you know the best weapon that is used to produce fears are your past failures, mistakes, and recorded falls? The children of Israel were so close to the promised land, but because of fear and how they saw themselves, caused many to die in bondage. They were bound by fear, even though they were close to the promise; never making it.

How many things do we have to be close to but not receive in order to face our fears? I believe that one of the greatest tools that the devil uses to break up marriages is the fear to love, forgive, and restore. This is why it is so important to know the truth about you and God because only the truth will free you, all else will keep you going around in circles.

Cursed by Love

Since my earliest memory, I wanted my natural father to love me. Something happened to me in the years that he and my mother were together. I remember the drama, when I was about five years old, about the lady next door, who was pregnant by my father while he and my mother were married. When my mother found out that she was pregnant by my father, she went next door and fought the lady, who was white; so you know that made my mother mad.

The lady lost the baby and, for some reason, that marked me. I also remember when my father hit my mother with a broom in the basement of our house. He had one of my arms and my mother had the other; they were fighting over who would take me. All of these kinds of things wounded me in knowing love. I loved and hated my father, but I also wanted to be just like him. When I got older I would say and think things like, "a white woman will treat you better," or I would say that, "if my mother didn't talk back so much and had learned to be silent like a white woman maybe I would not have lost my daddy." I remember saying to my mother that when they got a divorce, my dad also divorced me. It didn't help at all when she would remind me of all the girls my father had, and how he made good money; how he took care of his girls but we struggled very hard.

Now it may seem as though I was mad at my dad, but the truth is I was confused because of the stories and the circumstances that should have made me hate him. Yet, deep inside, I longed for him, still loved him, and could not understand why. This made me think that something was wrong with me to love someone that I had no apparent reason to love. Later in my life, this became a God-problem when He asked me to love people that hurt me or help people that abandon me. I would say "why me? Not again."

For years, I believed that I loved 'everybody' but no one really loved me. These thoughts began to curse me – pushing further from the people that I loved. See, my father did not come by very often (or even a little), but I associated him not seeing me, spending time with me or leaving me, as a sign that I could not be loved. My thought was I was wrong in wanting love or even expecting it. I became an unattractive person from within, which later on, made me always need affirmation.

I tell you the truth, when you need affirmation, praise and applaud, this can be one of the greatest drugs that you could ever be on. This can be the reason why you must have the best clothes, live in the best houses, and even be the 'best' in God. It's all from the drug called 'needing affirmation from man.' One of the main reason that Jesus' ministry was successful is because of when he was affirmed at baptismal and God said "this is My beloved Son, in whom I am well pleased." Nothing or anyone else could lift him up. Even when the devil tried to give Him all the kingdoms of the world, He still did not bow because He knew who He was.

But, when you have a need to be loved, you may sell your soul just for that feeling of belonging. There are many women and men who have lost their purpose and passion in exchange for so-called love. Trust me when I say that because I was one of them - who gave up preaching, music, and everything just to be loved by someone that was not designed to love me God's Intended way. That place is only for God himself. We must not replace affirmation with applause.

Okay, let's go back to my father not seeing or not spending time with me. This took on a form that went so deep that I thought no one really loved me, or could see the gift I had inside and my need to be loved. As a result, I did everything, and I mean almost everything, the good and the bad to get my ego stroked or my praise. MY PAIN SAID VERY LOUD "YOU WILL SEE ME. AND YOU WILL NOT DO ME LIKE MY FATHER." My mind was gone, lost in space with no place called home. I was only happy when I was preaching or playing music because life was too small for my problems. I thought I was cursed with this need to love but can't find love in return. Cursed to be committed not loving to commit.

Love for God Will Always Get Your Flesh in Trouble

Moses' trouble was leading the children of Israel out of bondage, and that brought trouble. Abraham was born to establish our faith but in order to do that he had to leave his family, and that brought trouble. So, trouble is the mission; love is the purpose; and God gives the assignment. Do we really love God enough that when trouble is the mission you say not impossible?

When I look at my life, I see the hand of the Lord on me in so many ways, but mostly in troubled times. I have cried, gotten mad, wishing to die, and then God asks, "Jenkins can I use you?" Well, there it is. I said, "yes" and then would go back to doing what He wants and truthfully, what I wanted too. But I just wished I could do it without the pain sometimes. I knew, from studying The Word, that He had chosen me before the foundation of the world and that my steps were ordered by the Lord. All things do work together for the good… and this must include trouble.

My calling brought trouble. I have been called an Apostle, (which means to many, a father), but God allowed me to be in a family where my father was not there. This worked to the plan of having an apostolic calling on my life -to be a spiritual father to many. Not having a father in my life created a void that would help me to know the importance of being there for my sons and daughters in the Lord. Sometimes it's the *lack* that reveals the importance of what is needed.

I used to say things like, "my father didn't give me much," but that's not true because his absence created a need to know God's Love as a Father. My pain, of not having my father in my life, blinded me so much that I ignored the good things that my father gave me just from his D.N.A. Things like the ability to laugh, to talk, his good looks, his musical abilities, and much more. But these things, also, were a wakeup call for me through the void in my life. My mother told me about God, but the need for a father *drove* me to God.

I heard a story about a man who was very hungry and went outside to grill a steak. He put the meat on the grill and went into the house to get something. While he was in the house, a dog came by and took the meat. Well, when he came back outside and saw that the steak was gone, he noticed the children were laughing, and saying, "I know you mad now to the point that you don't even want a steak!" The man said, "not so but I am really hungry and will eat two steaks tonight." It was the void and the loss of the steak that created a greater hunger. That's what God does in our life sometimes. Often, it's the problem that brings us to the answer - sickness that takes you to a doctor, and sin that brings us to a savior. If God's Biggest problems are people, His greatest concern is *for* people. He died, not for brick and mortar, but for flesh and blood. Look for God to trust you with His greatest treasure, and HIS GREATEST TROUBLES; they're called PEOPLE.

Trouble Should Bring You to Love

If you look through the Bible, you will see that people who were called and gifted were also trusted with trouble. Joseph has a dream, and then his brothers show him a nightmare. Peter says to Jesus, "you are The Christ," and a few verses down Jesus called him the devil. The trouble is sometimes the things that you know, the belief that you have, and the visions that you were given. My biggest trouble came when I started to see and believe what others wanted to ignore. Peter walks out to Christ on the water and there came a storm. If you really don't want trouble in your life, then stay in the boat, where it's safe, but I'd rather be walking *to* Jesus and almost drown than stay in a boat, never knowing trouble that comes from listening to God.

GM (General Motors), the car factory has a saying that goes, 'before it is driven it is tested.' Well, so does God. From the time I was born, God trusted me with trouble and not only trusted me but, also, has equipped me for it. I would say, "God why me?" "why my father?" and "why my mother?" God, then, would say, "why not you and your family? Would you rather I show my love through someone else?" God told me that the key to victory was in allowing me to depend on the unfailing word of God in my life. Paul says it this way: " I therefore, the prisoner of the Lord, beseech you that ye walk worthy of the vocation wherewith ye are called," (Ephesians 4:1) - and you must know and accept that trouble comes with your calling. I tell you no lie, it hurts, and it is painful to be trusted with trouble. The longer it lasts, the more you die and all of this is necessary.

When you don't understand God's Ways and His will, then time will become an enemy. But when you understand God's Love for you, time has become your friend. I cried for many years and was so confused about my purpose. Who wants to fail in marriage over and over again, and yet God tells them to learn from, and not carry the guilt from, it. There was so much trouble I received from not having a father. Many times, I was at the point of death. I had guns pointed at me, men trying to seduce me. I was pushed around at times and chose to cry rather than to kill, because of the anger that I had. I could have chosen to kill as well because my real troubles were the thoughts that wanted to be released. There would have been much more trouble had I been led by them.

Then, there was the trouble with betrayal that came from the people that I either played music with or trusted a lot. I had to start looking at these things from God's Eyes because my father was not the problem. The devil knew who I was, that was the problem. Maybe the devil was trying to make me believe that if I were not loved, not wanted, then maybe I would never believe what God has called me to. I hated that, after all that my father did and didn't do, I still loved him. I would ask God, "why I still love these people that hurt me so much?" "Why do I want to be married after being married so many times?" And my biggest question was "why do I still believe in love?" God said to me "because you are called to be like Me, and I am Love." He said to me, "why do I, as

God, keep loving sinners over and over again? Why do I keep forgiving over and over again, knowing that you will go and sin again? Because I love you, and love is the only way to restore and rebuild. These things are not about your marriage or your father. They're about my love shining *through* you." He said, "son stop looking for love and know that you *are* love. Until you get this, I will put you in places that will not love you back until you understand that you are not with them to get love but to *be* love. That is your life's calling."

The truth comes to make you free, and freedom is love. Build yourself unto God, and you will find yourself in Heaven, right here on Earth. When problems and passion increase, it's also when the revelation of trouble is discerned. In order to get through, there are things we must do to get to the place where we belong, and most of the time it's trouble that takes us there.

We must have an attitude that focuses on God and not the hate or the hater that may come your way. Love gives us the power to bless those who hate us. Remember, they hated Jesus who did no wrong. Can you handle the hate that comes with being anointed, or will you hold hate in your heart towards those that show this hate to you? Joseph, who had no problems with his brothers until he had a dream that seemed to placed him above them and until his father gave him a coat of many colors, brought jealously out in his brothers. The next thing Joseph knew was that he was put in a pit. And you will be hated for these reasons as well.

You will be hated just because of God's Favor on your life. I tell you this from my own life. Just deal with it, cry but deal with it1 Yes, you are pregnant, and the father of the baby is God. It's not your fault, but it is your responsibility that you've been chosen to carry the baby. Again, this is a plan of God; you can't get mad at what God allowed. You must be willing to pay the price for you to *know you* and to *be you*. Believe me, there is a price to pay! If you go to the store and buy a bottle of oil, the price may be $3.25, but if you ask the olive tree what it costs, it will tell you that it was a whole lot more. The cost to be anointed comes with living with trouble. If you are not ready for trouble then you are not ready to be used. I was told that an enemy is only a friend that has been wounded. So, can God trust you with a wounded enemy, called your pastor, father or family and you accept the call?

When Loving You is Killing Me

There were times in my life that I wanted love so badly that I would do anything to get it. One of the craziest things to do is to chase love, because you will never find it. The bad thing is, that if you caught it, you could only receive it in the way that you thought it should be. Most of the time, we only know love from our perception and not God's Expression. This became death to me, because I was losing who I was just to be happy, and then I was not happy because I was not myself. I was lost because loving them was killing me, and I thought, at the time, that it was their fault.

But later, God woke me up to how it was my own perception of love that was really killing me. Not only that, but because of a lack of self-love, I would always choose someone that was not right for me. I would only end up unhappy which would make them think that nothing that they did could make me happy. This was true because I didn't love myself enough. It's bad when I kill my passion for yours or kill my gift just to stand in awe of yours; always loving you and at the same time hating me, calling death love. Yes, death can bring us to love and yes, love will lay down its life; but when this happens in the right place, restoration or resurrection is around the corner. When love is being buried but the ground will not give a return, then love should take another look to see if this is really God, or lust in the name of love.

When Love for Another Replaces God

Many times, it's the need to be loved by a person that replaces God from being first in our lives. We begin to love other people and things more than God. Our humanity will allow people to become everything to us. We will even be fooled in our spirit about what we really want. Our needs will blind us to the point that we don't even care about God's Standards or anyone else's. We will begin to love people in an unhealthy way, to the point that we look to them to do things for us, that we were not even willing to do for ourselves. We will talk to them in ways that we never talk to God. These kinds of relationships become unlawful soul ties.

We are willing to give up everything to be loved by them. These relationships become our reason for living. We get married for other reasons than love. These relationships become our own dream and not the will and purpose of God. The problem is in how we allow this need to be loved by others to move God out of His place in our lives. I believe that the real problem is that we are only allowing God to hold that position until we believe we've found His kind of love and hope in others; thinking they will save us.

CHAPTER 15

Finding the Truth is More

Secrets cannot survive in an environment of truth and honesty. In fact, they aren't necessary. When I look at the story in **Luke 19:5-8** that says,

5. and when Jesus came to the place, he looked up, and saw him, and said unto him, Zacchaeus, make haste, and come down; for today I must abide at thy house.
6. And he made haste, and came down, and received him joyfully.
7. And when they saw it, they all murmured, saying, that he was gone to be guest with a man that is a sinner.
8. And Zacchaeus stood, and said to the Lord: Behold, Lord, the half of my goods I give to the poor; and if I have taken anything from any man by false accusation, I restore him fourfold.

This is a perfect example of when there in true intimacy, it brings honesty. Zacchaeus had been robbing the people for years with their taxes, but when Jesus went home with him without any pressure, the honesty came out. People want to be free but without the judgment that we, sometimes, bring when the real story is told. There is a difference between issues that are private and confidential verses those that are a secret - anything that is in the dark the devil has access to because he is the ruler of darkness. Private and confidential issues can be in the light yet only open to certain people. One of the troubles I was entrusted with was realizing that even trustworthy people can sometimes fail you.

     My first response was to withdraw from all people because a person had hurt me. We must always remember that hurt people hurt people and forgiven people forgive. We can never be free if we are not willing to be honest with ourselves. The first thing that God says to Adam is, "where are you?" When we are able to say where we are, even when we put ourselves in a position (place) called 'Lost,' it is then that help can lead us out. Can you honestly say where you are, why, and how you got there? Adam admitted his fears and why he was afraid.

     This is so painful because as long as we lie about where we are, we cannot be helped. Maybe, the truth is that we may not want help to get out, but just want someone to be concerned that we are in a mess! The real pain is that I am a preacher, teacher, and a man of God but naked and ashamed how I see myself. If you are lost, trying to get to a friend's house and you call them telling them that you are lost, the first question that they will ask you is, "where are you?" You can't get to where you are going, even when you are lost, if you can't say where you are. You, first, must be able to handle the truth about yourself. Being lonely of the mind is the first sign of separation and divorce. If the devil can convince you that you are missing something, then you will always be looking on the *outside* to receive what you *already have*.

In the Bible, a woman is the symbol of a well, and the man is a symbol of a fountain. They both carry water but they have different methods of giving out this water. The water must be drawn out or pushed and primed. The fountain water is under pressure and must be release by a foot release or a valve. So, whenever things don't work, always check why, because blame steals the energy to recognize the truth about what just happened. Are you low on water in your relationship and if so, then, why? Women, don't let every man draw from your well so that when your husband comes along, you are out of water.

Men. just because you are under pressure doesn't mean that everybody should drink. God did not say be "seed-full," but he said be fruitful. Which means stop placing your seed everywhere when you know that you are not going to be around to see it grow. This needs to be talked about as much as you're calling to preach. See. the reason why so many of us are out of control is that we lie about our sexuality and hide behind our call. Can you be truthful, without the need to be right? Trying to be right all the time will have you lying all the time.

In the Bible, the rich young ruler wanted to be right and said to Jesus, "good master, what do I have to do to have eternal life?" and Jesus' words were so real. He said, "there is none good but The Father, so why call me good?" Now that's keeping it real. But, then He said to him, "by keeping the Ten Commandments," and the rich young ruler said, "I have kept them since I have been young." Then Jesus hit him with the real test, "then go, sell all that you have, then give to the poor and take up your cross and follow me." The rich man who thought he was so right, left with his head down, knowing that his words had just betrayed him.

If we look at the first commandment, we will see that he was not real about that.

Exodus 20: 2-3

2. **I am the LORD thy God, which have brought thee out of the land of Egypt, out of the house of bondage.**

3. **Thou shalt have no other God's before me.**

Money had become his god, and just like many men in the ministry, money has become our God. Let's be honest about our real passion and still know that if God can handle my truth then so can I.

Can You Handle the Truth?

What if the truth is a lie that brings me success in my eyes? If my mother never really loved my father and my father is really not my father, but they stay together to get me in college… If my pastor is gay, but he loves children and was a great person to me.

What if the truth is that I make you laugh so that I will not cry about how bad my life is? The truth could be that I drive a new car but live with a broken heart. I preach life and, all the while, I wish that I were dead. If your pastor or preacher told you the truth could you still hear him preach? What if your favorite gospel singer told you that they get high right before singing and they love to look at naked pictures? In your eyes, are they now still anointed? Were they anointed because you didn't know the truth? Well, if this is hard for you handle, what about them? Just think how they see themselves. These are the things that keep us in the prison of our mind.

     We read about Peter, the Apostle, who denied Christ three times and David, a man after God's Heart, who had a woman's husband killed so that he could have her; or Apostle Paul, who while preaching, tells us that he is a chief sinner - still, we love these people of GOD BUT IF THEY WERE IN OUR LIFE OR OUR CHURCH, REALLY WHAT WOULD WE SEE? Until we can face our truth in our own life, we will never let others become free. The truth is that God created everything out of His Word, and all we need is a Word over our life. The truth is that it's not me that you see, but His Word over my life that qualifies me to be. That's the truth and nothing but the truth, so help me God!

The Truth About It All

Just like Christ who was wounded for us, I was, and you will also be, wounded for others. Even if it takes a wound to bring healing then, why not? If there is a problem, then there will be a cure. Everyone wants to be a cure but who is willing to suffer the lessons to know the cure? The truth is that strength comes out of the *struggle*. Anybody that has helped you, in any way, remember this, they had to be wounded for you. Some people learned at others' expense. We must have the will to serve and share the abundant life, which is available if we are willing to listen to our inner source and to translate our inner voice into vision and action.

We must remember that, apart from the mind of God, your purpose can never be completed. There is a great need to establish us in those things that are conducive to the prosperity from within. The greatest riches are the thoughts of Christ being lived on Earth. We must be honest about why we were in some confusion, because of the message that will come out later, and this will bring people to a better place in God. We fight to get out of problems so quickly, that we have not learned the lessons from the problems and why God allowed them in the first place. If you got to go to hell at least come back with some keys, and if you don't, you may repeat the class! Remember your suffering is not about you. Problems are the classes that we *all* must attend, and there will be a roll-call to make sure that you are there, but you were only called to the class to learn the lessons, not repeat them.

You Will Never Conquer the Promise, With a Grasshopper Complex

Remember, there is a difference between killing giants and ignoring them. Most of us rather ignore them, while feeding them, but the greatest giants to fight are from within. I thought I could still function as a blessing while thinking of my life as a curse. The unexamined life is not worth living *unexamined.* Why stay on a road that you're aware is a road of death or destruction? It took me many years to say, "I refuse to die an unlived life!" Life is about living, yet I wanted to die. Tell the truth to yourself, ask yourself these questions, "am I happy, or am I doing what I was born to do?" "Have I learned the lesson of life?" Remember that these foundational truths can't be moved.

Honesty

Can you talk to yourself without the dream, and without the lies? Can you say, "I am fat, greedy, and selfish" and if these things are hard, what about those things that are unseen to people? You know *YOU.* We rather be silent about things we don't want to lose. Silence could become your hiding place when it should reveal what you're hiding. The place of truth must, first, be in *you* before you tell it to others. It's a shame when we allow one thing to kill everything in our life. So be honest about the *one thing*, and you will see the *many things* show up. **The love for God must always be first in our life.**

The Truth Behind the Storm

Wake up, people of God and see the truth behind the storm! For the real truth is not a storm, but instead, it is the wind of God, speaking and saving us from ourselves and our wants. Things which would have enslaved us to the past pain and hurts that we kept repeating. God said, "No, not this time! I am setting you free from all your fears, failures, and fractured life. I have freed you, to fix you for good." Wow! What good news this is. We are free to finally *be*.

For me, this means no more doing things to prove who I am. No more lying to fit in a place where God says I am not wanted. My current circumstance is not a storm; no, it's my answer to the real prayer that was in my spirit. We wanted out of religion; we were tired of giving our body to a place where the heart of God was not. Ready or not, God came! So, I say to you "rejoice! for if God be for you who can be against you?" Stop fighting your promotion. Just because the mother is hurting while carrying the baby, doesn't mean that the baby is in pain. The baby causes the pain, but the baby is not in pain. Your so-called 'storms' are only your new baby saying, "it's my time to be born." Pain is only a reminder of how close the delivery is. It's a new thought, day, and a new way of being. This is the life that we have never seen before, so give birth to the new you.

*Say to yourself, I agree that God is the truth and nothing but the truth, for God has already helped me to be true to **me**.*

The Truth About Confessing

You get what you confess when what you are confessing is in the will of God. The vital key is confessing (or speaking aloud) and thereby, releasing the word of faith. It's by a mouth's confession that the faith power can be released. The key to receiving the desires of your heart is to release the Word of God out of your mouth and always be in agreement with Him. Whatever comes out of your mouth shall be produced in your life. Never make a negative confession: The tongue "can kill you, or it can release the life of God within you" - whether you believe right or wrong, it is still a spiritual law. There is power in your tongue. If you confess sickness you get it; if you confess health you get it; whatever you say you get.

Faith is as a seed that you plant by speaking it. The spoken word releases power for good or power for evil. Therefore, it is very important never to speak anything negative but only to make a positive confession. The 'Confession of Your Faith' should be what you live and walk by every day. Otherwise, the power of your own words can hold you in bondage. This is a spiritual law. I have learned the power of such a law as found in Mark 11:22-24.

It works every time and not just when it will be for your betterment.

Mark 11:22-24

22. And Jesus answering saith unto them, Have faith in God.

23. For verily I say unto you, That whosoever shall say unto this mountain, Be thou removed, and be thou cast into the sea; and shall not doubt in his heart, but shall believe that those things which he saith shall come to pass; he shall have whatsoever he saith.

24. Therefore I say unto you, What things soever ye desire, when ye pray, believe that ye receive them, and ye shall have them.

God never does anything without first saying it. This is readily observable throughout Scripture. We release our faith with words. These are called 'Spoken Words' because words are the most powerful vehicle for creation. Remember that words are seeds and they will always produce after their kind. Such is the law of the book of <u>Genesis</u> and is the principle behind seedtime and harvest.

Words are, also, containers, carrying either faith or fear. Words affect your spirit. A spoken word connects to your spirit, either for success or failure. Remember that you will plant God's Word in your heart much quicker by hearing yourself say it than you will by hearing is from others.

Building from Truth

If God has given me the power of my words, that can frame my world, then that puts the responsibility on what I say as well as what I would like to receive. Words are just like the ground they take, no responsibility for what you put in them. Their job is only to produce from the nature of what the word is and, just like the seed, the word is not responsible for the intent. So, I can speak positively, and I can also speak negatively. Knowing this should bring me to a place of responsibility, and I must become a seeker of truth. I cannot be irresponsible with the words I say. Why destroy life with the power of my tongue because I refuse to take the responsibility of seeking the truth that will make us all free? If the truth makes us free, then that means that a lie brings us into bondage. Why be responsible for bondage when I can be responsible for freedom?

The Truth Will Make You Free

God creates from the invisible, but He makes from the visible. Faith is the invisibly created material which is used to make the words spoken into visible material for use by all. Here is a side note (we will not stop lying if we stubbornly believe what we are unwilling to accept). It is very important that the spoken word is tied and married to truth. Whenever we speak something that is not the truth, we are now giving it permission to be on the same tree as truth -from the beginning God never wanted us to eat from the Tree of Knowledge of Good and Evil.

Trees are the symbol of righteous people, positioned in the *put place* of God. We should be like the tree planted by rivers of living waters. Water is, also, a symbol of the Word of God. "In the beginning was the Word and the Word was with God, and the Word was God." We also know that Jesus is the Tree of Life, so this means that the Tree and the Word are one, and the two together became flesh. This tells us that we should be planted in the spoken Word of God; not the bitter waters, but sweet-water from the Holy Spirit. We must speak the truth, those of us who have been awakened to the knowledge that we are trees. No more lies, no more can't, no more impossible. As it is in Heaven, that will I speak on Earth.

CHAPTER 16

Cracked Vessel - Fixed or Filled?

When you are on the journey of false perception, you find yourself playing the blame game. It's what Adam also did in the garden of Eden. The blame is the result of being a cracked vessel. Cracked vessels will crave other cracked vessels that want to be loved. Cracked vessels, always, blame the other for not doing what they need them to do. And if you do not know any better, they are easy to believe. This was my language as a cracked vessel for years. I would say, "I don't feel love, nobody loves me," and "I don't need friends because no one really knows how to be a friend to me anyways." Whatever you do is not enough. If you tell them I love you for three days in a row but on the fourth day you don't, here they come saying they don't feel love and guess what, in their perception they don't. This is the mindset of a cracked vessel.

A cracked vessel is someone that, regardless of what you do, you just can't fill them up. They have the house, the car, the dog, God and are still sad. It's bad when you are saved and sad, married and miserable. The worst is when you are cracked at the top. This is my story. I could almost be there and then something would happen. I could hold a lot of love, joy, peace but was just not able to get an over flow. I was this cracked vessel. It's very painful and it will have you asking, "God why? Why do I go so far and then fall? Go so high and then feel so empty? I can help so many others, but I am still starting over?"

The truth was that I was cracked from childbirth, not feeling love; cracked from bad preachers and teachers over me; cracked from bad relationships; cracked from bad choices. The real truth was that I was born a sinner and needed a savior in my life. Still, instead of asking God to fix me, I just went from one relationship to another, one church to another, blaming everything and everybody. Please remember God will only fill what He first fixes. Order always precedes the blessing. God is only asking you to be honest about your trouble because it's your trouble that leads you to His purpose in your life.

Bad Eggs Can't Make Great Omelets

You are who you are, so just be you! Remember, what was meant to be, will be. A person can become a bad egg when he or she is trying to be something other than what God made them. To yourself be true and always be true to you. Now the truth is, the wrong person can cause you to be someone other than yourself, and before you know it, you have lost yourself, lost your pride, your will to live and most importantly, your love and appreciation of self. Ask your friends to tell you the truth about yourself, especially when you were with someone that just did not fit. Please don't become a bad egg, and then hear them say that you don't taste right because you are trying so hard just to make them happy. You can't make people happy without becoming a prisoner to their needs. It's so easy to find faults in others but never see these same faults in yourself.

I had to learn how to be honest with myself and to admit that I was a mess. There were so many reasons for my false perceptions. I wanted to believe my own truth based upon the pain that I was giving myself. The crack that was in my vessel was because I believed what *I* wanted to believe, and I heard what *I* wanted to hear. A cracked vessel is the result of jealousy, and this mindset will never allow you to see the good in others before you get what you think is due to you first. Cracked vessel people always feel like they are over-looked and underpaid. This mindset will always have you with one eye open and one eye closed because, to you, others can't be trusted. Such thinking keeps you in defensive mode, making it hard to be authentic because cracked vessels have characteristic issues. Family become enemies when your soul is leaking. The bad part about this is that the person can't see their cracks. They may even say to you, "now what have I done, can't I even speak the truth?" All the time they are living a lie.

This leaking is embarrassing because it robs you of courage. You may even refuse to submit to counseling and any advice. Being a cracked vessel is like cancer and can become a silent killer. It may not even give anyone the right to speak their opinion. Cracked vessel people lose heart because they believe that people have lost heart with them. This is not the case, but their blindness to their own problems block the truth from coming in. In my own experience, and by what I have seen in others, many cracked vessels are anointed, strong, and intelligent but still. cracked.

These cracked vessels have real strong beliefs and you must cross every 't' and dot every 'i' or they will not hear you. Such a level of false perception is very dangerous; it also leads to some major behavior issues. Your mind is a very strong thing and when it believes something, often it takes God himself to break you free. The hard part about a cracked vessel is that you can't kill what you can't identify. Most people are not aware that they are cracked or where in their emotions the crack exists.

People who have been cracked have experienced a great amount of stress, which broke their heart by receiving unnecessary demands on it. Many of these demands came from the vessels themselves. The heart crumbles under the pressure that was not assigned to us by God. God puts no more on us than we can bear but often, we do. Many times, we fail to recognize the power that has been made available to prevent anxiety. The bad part about false perception is that all of your truth is really in your mind. One of the main revelations about mindsets is that they are actually laws in the mind that we believe and live by. They become strongholds and, many times, people defend their enemy unknowingly. This concept is very common in cracked vessels.

Finding the Rich Man on The Inside

Here are some questions that I want you to answer and I believe this will begin your journey to finding *you*. To help get you started with some examples, remember, when I am talking about *your name*, this is really not a name but a character that you represent on the earth but that comes from On High. For instance, my name from God is Love, this is what I should be named for on earth but my natural name is Robert James Duvall Jenkins. When I ask about the place you were born in question 2, I'm referring to the place in the spirit *and* in the natural. For me, I know that I was chosen before the foundation of the world but in the natural, it was in the back seat of a car. In the natural, I thought that my birthplace was cursed but in the spirit realm, I am blessed. But which one do we really believe when we look at our answers?

1. What are your names: the name from God and then the name from man? Which name is most important? Which name has the most power over you?

2. Where were you born, and did it have any meaning to your purpose? The place that you were born down here and the place you were born up there.

3. Is the name that man gave you really who you are or is this just your name on earth? Do these things define you or describe you correctly?

4. If your name were different, would you still be the same person?

5. Can I know you by your name?

6. Can I watch the way you act and if I call you by what I see, will you answer?

7. Are you what you see or what I believe about you?

8. Are you delivered from people's opinion of you and if so, how did you get free?

9. Do you believe what you want to believe and not what may be the truth?

10. If a name is a word that we use to identify something, then how important is your name to your character?

11. Why is your name given before your character is developed?

12. Could naming you also be molding you? If you give power to the name, before your character has power, then what is the consequence?

So, for example when they called you 'dumb,' was that before you had a chance to call yourself smart and if so where is the real problem? Is it in what they said about you or what they did not say about you? And do you call yourself something that you don't see?

13. Do you see to believe, or do you believe to see? And if you believe to see, then is that lying until the truth comes?

When we see the truth from the inside, the outside will change to what we see. Remember, that God's Chosen People lost the promise of the land because of how they saw themselves. A grasshopper complex will destroy the ability to walk into the promises of God. When you change the limits on whom you *be*, then you will remove the limits on what you can *do*. When Jesus broke the bread, the miracle was not the breaking of the bread – it was the breaking of the limitation that was on the bread.

Find who you are *(be)*, and then doing will be easy. This is a principle for the mind. The rich man on the inside is waiting for you to believe in him. The greatest wakeup call is when you answer the call from within. You are rich beyond measure, but you must believe this deeply for the baby in you to leap. False perception robs you of your true worth and value. False perception always tells you how broke you are and never is willing to reveal your true riches.

You are rich on the inside for your family and the nation. As long as you are being deceived by pain, many others will suffer. Do not allow your past or present pains to cause you to ignore this rich man. He is rich with wisdom, knowledge, and power but he must be released. God put him on the inside so that things on the outside will not shape or destroy him. The Bible says in,

2 Corinthians 4:7

7. But we have this treasure in earthen vessels that the Excellency of the power may be of God, and not of us. This treasure is God himself in us.

When we deny the rich man, we are really denying God. By yielding to the help from God in removing us from false perceptions then the truth of how great God is, in us, can be found. Why live a broke and miserable life when what we need to enjoy life to the fullest is in us?

This is why you need to answer all of the previous questions because you must know who you really are. You must remove all false perceptions, false titles, false images and get down to the real man on the inside.

CHAPTER 17

Thoughts from The New Landlord

One of the main reasons why people are in bondage is because they have not learned how to guard their thoughts (protect the land) which is very important to spiritual growth. Guarding thoughts is the same as having a security system in your house in order to know when someone is breaking in. When studying all problems that concern us, our search should be to find their roots and then pull them up. I have learned that most physical ills are now considered to be psychosomatic in origin, so we must begin to face the possibilities that most problems may be the outer manifestation of inner states of consciousness.

People have come to believe that the problems that they are facing are in what they see. For example, we think that money will solve all things. But the Bible says that the love of money is the root of all evil. Not money but *the love of money* and wherever there is love there is also a god. Therefore, we must, also, begin to declare our independence from the belief that our personal (inner) welfare is completely tied to the economic fluctuation of the world out there. We must begin to accept our responsibility of being disconnected from God (i.e. the fall of Adam), and know what this fall did to the world. This is because we are so weak and poor in the most important area of our lives, our mindset.

The Bible says that whatsoever a man thinks, so is he. So, real prosperity is a way of thinking and living. Prosperity is the whole experience of a healed life, fulfilled love, abiding peace, and harmony. Remember, that it is your mind that sets all limits in life. You are only so-called 'poor' on the outside, because you have not found out how 'rich' you really are from within. The starting point in realizing prosperity is to accept the responsibility for your own thoughts.

Here are Some Thoughts to Bring into Captivity

Place is the space that is occupied by the ruling thoughts of your mind.

I Can't

The voice of 'I can't' is only trying to stop you from hearing the voice of 'I have'. Remember that darkness is only in a place because light has not begun to shine. 'I can't' is trying to announce your weakness because strength has not been revealed. The word revelation means to uncover, not to create. The strength to do this is there, you just need to uncover it and see what God has already provided.

When I was a young man, I loved to watch the show called The Price is Right. This show had so many spiritual points to it. First, the people who were picked to play the game were people who were in the seats. Secondly, you had to be able to look at something and determine the price. The closest person to the price, without going over, would get to see what was behind the curtain.

Well, this is all GOD! Just stay with me for a minute… First point, God has chosen us from the seats of sin. Second, He has given us discernment to know the price of His blood (through Jesus Christ), and then He will show us the revelation of all the things that He has placed in us before the foundation of the world. But these things you will never see if you come to the table of life saying, "I can't."

Now, let's look at this same word from the positive side. We must remember that God is our example in all things. Well, you may not agree with this but there are some things that even God *can't* do. God can't lie, God, also, can't fail, and God can't lose. Well, if there are some things that God can't do that are positive then there are some things that I will not do that are positive as well. I will not give up on what God said because He can't lie. I will not give up on what God is doing because He can't fail. And I will not give up in this fight because God is in me and He can't lose.

Remember, all of these things must be received in your mind in order to remove the false perceptions that you believe. The mindset of 'I can't' has destroyed and held many great people in bondage naturally or even the greatest prison which can be that of your mind. The Bible says in:

Philippians 4:13

¹³ I can do all things through Christ who strengthens me.

If "I can do all things through Christ who strengths me," then the mindset that says that 'I can't do' is working without Christ. As long as we are connecting to the Christ mindset we *can* and we *will* stand. The old landlord or old mindset is full of 'I can't.' Let go and let God show you the truth about *you* and all that belongs to you. The old landlord was a liar and a taskmaster. He never wanted you free to be who you are. Until we walk in the light of truth we will be bound to this landlord. But Christ came to set us free; to enjoy peace and love, not guilt and shame.

CHAPTER 18

I Am Afraid

This voice tries to make you back up from love; it is a master builder of walls. The only one that can talk to this voice is the Voice of Love, because this voice speaks from reality, which is where his strength is. But, we must live by faith and faith works only by love. Where there is fear there is a lack of love.

When I looked back over my life, I was so amazed of how much fear I was operating in. I was so afraid of so many things, the good and the bad. I was afraid of what I could *not* do as well as what I *could*. I was even afraid of hearing some thoughts that I was thinking, out loud so I never spoke them, but I did think them. My biggest fear was the very thing that I preached about the most - truth. In all my preaching I talked the most about being true and how much Christians lie. But the truth was that so was I. I talked about being in relationships and being honest, but I was not honest with myself and didn't tell people everything because I was afraid of the loss but actually, I was already lost to myself.

Boldness to Face and Courage to Stand

Face your fears with faith and all your dreams will come true. Fears from your emotion will fight your faith that comes from your spirit. You can't run from your fears; you must walk right past them into your victory. Every great man in the Bible was told to "fear not" and "take courage" in order to fulfill their purpose in life. Knowing your purpose and God's Vision for your life will give you more control over it. Remember, that self-control is a fruit of The Spirit.

There is a time in your life when you will start to demand personal growth and empowerment to move ahead of your past. This is the pathway to finding yourself. It took me a lot of falling to learn that doubt, discouragement, and depression result from the lack of knowledge of the greatness we have within ourselves.

Suffering is Giving

Genesis 22; 1-18

[1.] and it came to pass after these things, that God did tempt Abraham, and said unto him, Abraham: and he said, Behold, [here] I [am].

Believe me when I tell you this, it will come to pass that your faith will be tested, and it will not be the devil but God Himself. A test is given to reveal to your faith where you really are and to show you that the teacher believes that you have learned the lessons in the class of life. When God is testing you, remember that it is only a test. It's not the end result of your life. God will never give you a test that He has not already given you the answers for.

Whenever God calls you to a test, remember to say, "here I am." Always be willing to be honest about the place you are at when testing time comes. Be willing to talk about where you are as well. The I AM is the God on the inside of all of us. Always bring your I am to the test (the I am is the spiritual man).

Genesis 22:2

2. and he said, Take now thy son, the only [son] Isaac, whom thou loves, and get thee into the land of Moriah; and offer him there for a burnt offering upon one of the mountains which I will tell thee of.

The test is to give back the promise that was given to you. It is difficult to give back something that you love and also that you waited a long time for or something that came out of your loins. But you can do it and remember, that the one who is asking you for it gave it to you in the first place. God will test you to see if your passion for a thing is greater than the passion you have for Him. Usually the very thing that God gives us is also the very thing that makes Him jealous because we begin to love the thing more then we love Him. Moriah means the bitterness of Jehovah - this is where change takes place in the consciousness, and this a very bitter experience. A strong faith is needed to believe that good will come of this. The sacrifice is needed but the right mountain is required for the blessing.

Genesis 22:5

5. And Abraham said unto his young men, Abide ye here with the ass; and I and the lad will go yonder and worship, and come again to you.

Even during the test, still worship The Father. Worship is the place where faith and clarity see; when storms are at their best.

Genesis 22:6

6. And Abraham took the wood of the burnt offering, and laid [it] upon Isaac his son; and he took the fire in his hand, and a knife; and they went both of them together.

Always be prepared to finish the test.

Genesis 22:7-8

7. And Isaac spoke unto Abraham his father, and said, my father: and he said, here [am] I, my son. And he said behold the fire and the wood: but where [is] the lamb for a burnt offering?

When Abraham spoke to God he said, "here I am," but when Abraham spoke to his son he said, "here am I."

8. and Abraham said, my son, God will provide himself a lamb for a burnt offering: so they went both of them together.

Abraham knew that it was God that provided him a son, and the same God that provided him a son would also provide a lamb. The same God that gave you what you have, also, can give Himself what He needs. So, the truth is that we are never giving God something that He lacks. We give not because He lacks but because He asked.

Where Do I Go?

Because I had been sitting so long complaining, I had lost my ambition and drive. I had no vision and there was no hope; all my thoughts were in despair. I let my past look down on me so much I started to enjoy sitting as a victim and not moving in victory. I thought fear had me when I was sitting, but it was really bad when I tried to move out of it or take a step in the right direction. The question for me was, "where to go now, when nothing is holding me?" I was like the children of Israel that prayed for 400 years to be freed from Pharaoh. But when God opened up the Red Sea, drowning their enemies right in front of them and left no enemy to blame, they still complained and were fearful.

I had allowed time to become my enemy. When people said to me, "give it time, be patient," I would say, "time is my enemy because, at the end of the day, I will be left alone; no one really cares about me." All I am doing is giving people time to show me what I already knew. This was my victim story about time. Time revealed where my faith was; time proved that it was not really faith at all.

I was given everything I needed in eternity but did not want to wait for it to be released by time. I was afraid of my future because I judged it according to my past. If I failed before, why should I believe that I would not fail again? If the first wife left me, why would anybody stay with me? See, fear always tries to tell you a logical answer to make you believe that your reasoning is true. But the truth really is that you are afraid. Your love is not perfected in that area. I didn't know how to move in love, I only knew how to stay in fear.

I'd been in fear for so long, to the point that God's Direction for my life was not clear because I believed that my record had destroyed my destiny. "Who will hear a preacher teaching about marriage, knowing that he has problems with staying married himself?" I said to myself. "Jenkins you have too many strikes in your life." I said, "Robert you are just like Moses, and because of your sins you will not make it to the same place that you helped others get. Even if you could be a blessing to someone, how can you get there? You know that in order to be famous, you must be gay, willing to control people or pay your way up. You are so transparent and want people to know the truth. You are doomed."

As I sat in the jail of my mind, thinking about my life, there were many questions that I hid behind my problems. See, my prison was in my mind and it was created by my own thoughts. The real bars were fears that I had about myself that I was unwilling to face. The angel did not only come to set me free, but he came to show me that the outside bars were not the problem. If I did not seek for the answers of the questions in my mind, then wherever I go I would take these bars with me. The biggest of those questions were the same fears that I've always had, "Will they love me for me? Will they leave me if they know the truth about my past? Can they love me after they know and experience my demons?" These visions were good but painful because I had to come out of it and answer these questions. I had no more excuses because I saw it and I saw me. Now what do I do? Who can I blame now?

Fear Holds Back Your Transition

After not being true to yourself for so long or helping others with their ministry so that when it comes to your turn, it's so amazing how you question yourself. The question that I asked myself over and over again was could I really do this? Then I would tell myself why I can't do it. This is because of all the so-called failures in my life. I let my age become a factor, my race, and questions like am I educated enough? Have I been married too many times? I was like the children in the wilderness when God had promised them the land of Canaan, but they saw themselves as grasshoppers.

The fear of failure and rejection was controlling my life. In my private time, when I was by myself, I knew what I could do. And when it came to spiritual things, I knew what God would do through me. But in the natural, I was very afraid of a lot of things. GOD became my only way out. I could preach from the unknown and trust GOD all the way. But I was afraid to even do my own income taxes! And as I became older, fear became stronger.

I used fear as a protector and I used knowledge to hide my fears. See, if I let you get rid of my fears then you might see me in the way that I really saw myself and that was not good at all. Fear became my Red Sea, which said I couldn't get out, and I will never cross over. Fear told me that it would drown me first before it would let me leave. Fear said to me, "your best message will never be heard, and your best song will never be sung. You will never have children and never be respected. You will die alone just like your mother, and your father is on his way." Well, what do you say to all this when this is how your reality looks?

 *"For God hath not given us the spirit of fear; but of power, and of love, and of a sound mind." (2 Tim. 1:7)*

This is a great Bible verse, but can we live here?

Who, among us, can say that he or she has not felt fear? I know of no one who has been entirely spared. Some of us experience fear to a greater degree than others. Some are able to rise above it quickly, but others are trapped and pulled down by it; even driven to defeat. I had seen the best fall under the spirit of fear which exposed the truth about them. Remember, the only way to leave fear is to go *through* it.

Fear the Wall of Hindrance

When we suffer from the fear of being ridiculed, it will cause us to lie, hide and some have even killed when pushed hard enough. When I think about the story in the Bible, about King Saul and how the people began to say that David was a greater warrior and how, from that point on, Saul began to hate the very one that he had loved so much. Fear will breed jealousy and the Bible says that love is as strong as death, and jealousy is as cruel as the grave; which hath a most vehement flame. I believe that the greatest wall to our success is fear. Fear cannot be out-run, so you must embrace it, go through it. Let me tell you a good secret: fear is not trying to only hide you but also hide what is yours on the other side of your Red Sea.

      Fear will use failure as a reminder of the past, in order to keep you there. Fear will use loneliness, to cause you to compromise. Fear will try to keep you in ignorance, just to make you a liar. Some of us carry the burden, guilt, and shame of sin. We'd give almost anything to unshackle ourselves from those burdens and fears that have changed our lives. We must recognize that fear does not come from God, but rather, that this gnawing, destructive element comes from the adversary of truth and righteousness.

      Remember now, that fear is the adversary of truth, that alone should tell you something. Fear is the antithesis of faith. It is corrosive in its effects, even deadly. *"For God hath not given us the spirit of fear; but of power, and of love, and of a sound mind."* Fears rob us of our strength and sometimes knock us down to defeat. I was afraid of saying I had a divorce and it took me years just to be honest about the things that happened in my life. The truth is that there is a mighty strength that comes from the knowledge that you and I are sons and daughters of God. Within us is something of divinity. Those that have this knowledge and permit it to influence their lives, will not stoop down to the fears that try to control them.

      The place where I lived was in fear of telling the truth because who would use me or let me preach if I told them the truth? Who would believe the revelation of God after knowing my life behind closed doors? People ask me, "how do you know so much?" Well, from being raised in a home that loved God by day, but also prostituted by night the same preachers that preached with me. My mother's best friends were pimps and preachers. My first drum set was stolen from my own cousin's church. I have great friends in God, but drug dealers and pushers were better friends.

My greatest example of love came from a man who was my stepfather, who struggled with homosexuality. It was he, not my natural father, who took me to church. He played the piano and I played the drums. He put my first piano and organ in the living room so that I could play all night with no restriction. My first musical partner was the gay guy who loved me like no other. But remember now, my father played the guitar but I was about 25 years old before he heard me play live. Who could I tell about my father who was a man's man? The man that I never knew until God healed our relationship. Or my stepfather, the gay guy, who knew how to love a boy when he wanted to be a woman.

See, it's taken years for me to learn that one of the core fundamentals of personal development is your thinking. The ability to change the way you view things in order to have a more successful life. My thinking had been challenged all of my life, like about a mother's real love. I remember getting married for the first time and the night before the wedding, me and my brother were about to fight so my mother said she wasn't coming to the wedding. With tears in her eyes she said, "you just don't know what I had to do to help pay for this wedding."

She was my mother. Some said she had sexual problems too, I don't know but others said she was a madam. Well, let me say it like this - pimps, prostitutes, thieves and many other things were not a stranger in my house. I was so gifted, confused yet afraid to tell, can you feel me?

CHAPTER 19

Recovery

Some Words to Speak and Eat Every Day

These are words and thoughts that I repeat every day. Now the reason why this lesson is so important to living is because most of us will only survive *and not* live or have life. We live incomplete and unfulfilled. The only way to return to your original self is to, first, acknowledge and pronounce who you really are, and this takes vision.

When I was young I loved to put puzzles together and one of the ways to do this well is to look at the picture on the outside of the box, and then find your corners and from there begin to put the pieces back together based on the picture or vision that you saw. Well, this is the same way in life - we must know the picture as much as the pieces. Connection comes when pieces are put together to match the picture that God Himself created.

You Can Do This

God has given us the Power of Truth

We must learn to believe in the power of truth over our own reality which is really based on our perception and understanding. This is why God says not to lean on your understanding but in all your ways let Him direct your path. My reality says, "because I have no schooling in ministry that I am not qualified" but the Bible says that before we were in our mother's womb we were chosen. We must apply God's Truth to our reality in order to do what God has equipped us to do. False perception robs you of knowing the power of truth that you carry. You will be surprised at how much you can believe and support others but think little of yourself.

By faith, in the Word of God, and by grace that was given to you, the assignment is done. Stop doubting yourself and start believing in what God has declared. If you would just step back and look, you will see that, somewhere in your life, you have and are doing these things. You were born for this, you were trained by God so get up and do it!

God would not have given you the dream if He didn't want you to carry it out. The key here is to understand how to move with God's Timing and not give up before the miracle happens. God is a God of recovery and equipping. It's time to let God's Glory expand and enlarge every part of our being. We are called to see, know, and become the way of the light and not to belittle ourselves and to think small.

CHAPTER 20

The Picture of Your Life

God is my instant, constant, and abundant source of supply. When we say these things remember you are activating what God has always been declaring, and what you have always believed. When you say that God is instant, you are reminding yourself that you already have what you need. When you say that God is constant, you are really saying that God will never leave you to yourself. And when you say that God is your abundant source of supply, you are really saying that you can never be in need or lack.

God has put ideas into my mind, words into my mouth, and creativity into my hands. These ideas are for our now and later journeys. They must leave our minds and flow out of our mouths, then be worked by our hands. We are to bring those ideas up every chance we get and believe in them, cultivating them like plants in a garden. Remember, the most power is in our mouth, so speak what you see. When it comes to our creativity we are limitless. One of the main reasons why you don't see some things that you think are needed on the earth is because you have not spoken it into this realm yet.

I will always be moving in the direction of my dreams. This is something that you must keep on your mind, at all times. The biggest threat to your enemy is your dreams being reviewed and renewed on a daily basis. Remember that these dreams are the things that are on God's Mind and He is using you to bring them to pass.

I will talk only about the things that I want to see live and grow. This will bring control over your emotions and give you responsibility over your words. This takes a lot of self-control and a death to self because our very nature loves drama.

My thoughts are the previews of the coming attractions. This is the reaping of what you sow principle. If your thoughts have the power to bring to you what you *think*, then the real power should be in what you *think* and not in what you *receive*.

God's Thoughts are words, but God's Words are pictures. This means that when God speaks to you, you can see what He said. So, here is the Spiritual Law: God's Thoughts become words. His words become pictures and pictures become reality. If this is a Spiritual Law, then never allow man's reality to become your pictures and man's pictures to become your words or your words will become your god. Having God's Words out of order is also having you out of order.

The word of God is how eternity crosses over into time. This means that eternal words will be released in a time zone when you speak them, but they will also last forever. This is why, when we speak these things, we wait for God's Timing to reveal what He said.

My first intercourse is with faith and God's Word. This means that every moment of the day I should be pregnant with a word from God because we live and walk by faith and His Word. But remember that faith comes by hearing and hearing by the Word of God. Therefore, we repeat these words that God put in our spirit and allow our spiritual ears to hear them as well.

Warning!

 *These things must be practiced before they are preached. Do not be over read and under done.*

The Original

One of the most important questions in life is who are you? Can you define yourself? Is it possible to know who you are, by yourself, or do we need someone to tell us? Or is that the job of our parents? What if our parents don't know who *they* are? What happens when the people in our lives are wrong about the identity of who we are? Then, are we lost forever? After we find out about who we are, and we don't like that person, are we stuck?

I know these are great questions and, believe it or not, they may take a lifetime to answer. And the truth is that it's not really about the answer as much as it is about the search and the journey. How wrong is it for you not to be you? Did you know that the first suicide was when Adam ate from the Tree of Knowledge of Good and Evil? That caused him to hide from God, (which was really running from himself, The Original). Most of our lives, we are trying to be someone else, trying to please family, friends, husband, wife. But who are you?

When I think about the story of the prodigal son, I question was he lost because he left home or was he lost to himself, because "when he came to himself" that's when he went home. Home is where love is and The Father. We can never come home unless we find ourselves. Whenever The Father gives you a blessing to leave, then you know that the experience of the journey must be greater than the blessing, and the real blessing is not the monetary inheritance or whatever, but it is the spiritual inheritance of coming to know whom you (The Original) really are.

There is nothing that we have been through that God couldn't have stopped. Then why did He allow it? He knew that we would be conformed to the image of Christ.

Love will always allow you to grow into yourself.

CHAPTER 21

The Result of a Disconnection

One of the greatest lessons that I had to learn was that I belong to a purpose, which includes people as well. If the enemy could get me to disconnect from people, then my purpose would be lost. There was a great reason why my father was who he was and a great reason why my mother was who she was in my life. The enemy tries to show us the negative side of our life to influence us from God's Purpose and plans for it. As I said before, if the environment is not one for the seed then it doesn't matter how powerful or how much potential the seed has, the environment will restrict its growth. This is the same case for people that remove themselves from purpose or people. This disconnection changes the atmosphere or the temperature of the house.

A disconnection in a marriage can cause a house not to become a home. There are some very painful things that result from being out of place even when it looks right. The real pain is when things that looked right make room for the disconnection, exposing the nakedness and shame that was hiding behind false success. One of the reasons why we see a great disconnection is because of the other voices that are in our head that have become ruling thoughts; these thoughts will dominate our life. Satan is an opportunist and he will take advantage of every opportunity that he can.

The Fruits of Wounded People

One of the first signs of wounded people is their inability to develop trust in another, which leads to a constant sense of insecurity. The mind is strange sometimes, but very practical and it tells us when we are wounded that, in order to not be wounded again, don't trust. Pain and wounds will always point you to where the pain came from and never prepare you to handle it. After you become wounded, you also become weak. If you never deal with what was weakened, then you begin to find a place to hide that weakness.

This mindset makes it hard to receive love. The person may love you but, because of your lack of trust, you may never connect to them even though they have connected to you. When you are insecure, it will always create an environment that makes it look like you have a reason to not trust. When trust is wounded it brings a mindset that makes you afraid of being vulnerable to being hurt or subjected to pain. This vulnerability removes the possibility of being loved, because love is all about risk and vulnerability. The real problem is that the Bible tells us to trust no man, and, also, have no confidence in the flesh. See, we try to depend on man in places where only God can be dependable.

Another fruit of wounded people are the walls that they set up to protect their insecurity, which walls really are nothing but a prison we put people in to prove that they love us; or a place where we can see them at all times so that we think, now, we are safe with them or they respect us. Truth is, *we* just become a prisoner.

When you are wounded, the wound itself will give you a spirit of rejection and that spirit or mindset will have you say or even do some things that you never even thought was a part of you. This mindset of rejection is, sometimes, allowed in our life by God to show us the other side of us that we have ignored for so long.

There are things in us that we need to talk about, things that we need to be real about. What is better - a mad truth or a glad lie? Remember now that truth sets us free but lies bind us in the ground and then look for ways to bear fruit.

How to Break the Circle of Broken Relationships?

It is necessary to develop a God-confidence in your ability to handle a relationship, *and I mean a God-confidence and not a man-confidence.* When you have been broken and robbed by the pressures of life, your true identity is lost, relationships will become your way or no way. I was so wounded by life and by circumstances, that led to many divorces and suicide attempts.

One of the ways that God has helped me through is counseling. Receiving Godly counseling from a person that will not confuse your gift with your character. In Luke 4:18 Jesus says that He was anointed to heal the brokenhearted. It takes the anointing to bring healing to the brokenhearted. I had to sit under the anointing and allow the Holy Spirit to take me back to the place where I first believed and received the love of Jesus Christ, because brokenness had kept me at the place where I was broken, replaying the tape of my past over and over again.

You have to begin to believe in *your God-worth* and know, without a shadow of doubt, that you *are* who *God says you are*. The purpose of the enemy is to put you under a false covering or false perception using your truth in them (the enemy) and to kill, steal, and destroy. I was so bad that I was putting my worth in the hands of women, marriages, church, gifts and many other things, all to define me. I only came to God when what I wanted and thought I needed from them did not work. But the truth was that I lacked true identity and that lead me to the physical manifestation of where I was already.

Let go of your fears or you'll never embrace love to its fullness. Fear will control every expression of true love and freedom. The power of fear is in the memory of our reality. Our reality will always justify fears' reasoning. There are some things in life that belong to God even in the earth realm, like love and trust.

The Bible is very clear on these subjects. For instance, when it comes to love its says, "to love God with all your heart, soul, and mind." Which, if this is done, then you have no love of your own to love man with, which is very safe. For love is too strong for the human character to handle or even practice. God is the only one that can contain love. Who can really say that they can suffer all things, or endure all things? These are the characteristics of God. But, we try to love like this without being dead to our emotions or will. When we are offended (because results or expectations are not fulfilled the way we expect them to be) , we bail out or blame others. These feelings may lead us to believe that we were betrayed, when really the truth is that we were asking something from man that only God can give.

This is really what happened to Judas in the Bible and what also happens to many great leaders in life. The power of betrayal is powerful - betrayal is one of the hardest things to overcome, and the only healing to face the pain and the one who betrayed you, is to love God enough; to love in pain. It may take crying, sometimes, while practicing the very thing that you can't feel but it's the only way back to health, which is spiritual warfare in the flesh. In others words, you may have to do what is right while feeling all the wrong until the truth is revealed about the heart of the one who wounded you. Do not focus on the wound.

I have a friend who was married, and her husband cheated on her and this hurt her really bad. But she believed that God ordained her marriage, so she forgave him after some time, following their breakup and separation. Her husband returned home, and they began to make love again. She said that the first time was so hard to let him touch her, after knowing where he had been. But she also knew that if she didn't let him, their marriage could not be totally restored. She explained that she cried all night while making love to him, but she had to, in order to restore her marriage and his betrayal. While making love to him she said to herself, "*I am able and willing to overcome this problem.*" Her tears were the manifestation of the emotional pain she was going through, but she kept moving forward through the pain.

Moving forward, through the pain, is very painful but rewarding in that it helps you overcome betrayal. But even this cannot be until there is time in between the wounded and the one that caused the wound. The Bible says that, in patience, you possess your soul. Anytime that there is a broken heart and a ripping of the soul it will take time (which is patience), to get your soul back whole. Time brings enough healing to the wounded, so they are able to start the healing process with the one that caused the wound.

A main reason why betrayal is so hard to overcome is because we put trust in man when we should put trust in God. The Bible says to trust no man (Psalms 118:8), and to put no confidence in the flesh (Philippians 3:3). People who put their trust in relationships and experience betrayal take on a mindset that I call 'habitational mistrust', which means that now there is an ongoing thing - either they never trust or in every relationship they try to trust again and fail. The blame will always come out, as no one can be trusted, and a real bad case of self-guilt and shame.

The truth is that healing is needed and then a mature growth in God and from this one learns to trust Him and never (to trust) the flesh. I hope that these lessons will help you have knowledge of the required attributes of a healthy relationship. I lost many things so that you may not have to, so please, pay attention because I paid the "cost to attend" these lessons so you wouldn't have to – know it cost me a lot!

Strongholds

I am very aware of strongholds. Strongholds in my family are very real -from diabetes, sexual immorality, fornication, adultery, killing, and witchcraft. The reason I've been through so much was to recognize these strongholds and become a help to others. We are not here for ourselves - we are here to show God's Love to others, through sacrificial love. The questions to ask in any relationship are, "what can I see? What looks like me? or looks like the way I was?" I could blame everyone for what I thought they did wrong but really, what was in them was also in me. Magnets can only draw others' magnets. You bear fruit of your own kind.

Do you think that God just goes around telling and showing you things about people for no reason? Do you believe that God just allowed you to make a fool of yourself for kicks? I believe that every one of my relationships was for purpose but, because I was in so much need, I married my ministry, my friends and my pain (The need to please the flesh will darken your mind). Not everybody is your wife. We do marry our ministry, and what I mean by this is that we marry the persons that we should have ministered to in some way, but we end up ministering from the flesh and not from the spirit. We were in their life to help them with their strongholds but instead, we *become* their stronghold. The purpose of this, all, was to help them.

Can You Trust Unlawful Soul Ties?

One the greatest distractions is the going down of God's Light. The Bible says that we are the light of the world, but what can you do when the light of God is going dim because of the relationships you are in? I had to learn that soul ties could hurt so many people especially when we don't want to kill our flesh. It's bad when soul ties will have you sleeping with members of the church, with people who trusted in your anointing, cheating in your marriage. These lessons should bring us to a place of honesty about the wickedness of our heart and make us aware of the attacks on our lives. It also should show us the strength of bondages when you are not honest. God wants us to value His Word more than our needs. But, most of the times we rather take care of our needs and then say we value The Word.

When I look at David's life in the Bible I see a man who seemed to have it all together. He could write songs to God and he killed Goliath the giant but he also had a soul tie with another man's wife and God allow it and allowed us to read about it. One of his requests, in prayer, was for God to restore his soul. See, trouble is designed to bring you to the truth about you. Sometimes, soul ties are hiding places for weakness and undeveloped people.

In Matthew 19:12-18 Jesus talks about eunuchs that are made for the kingdom of Heaven. We can be so delusional that we think we're doing the right thing and giving up the right things but, at the same time, it was because we were not honest about where we were. And then we chose to make ourselves eunuchs, not for the kingdom of Heaven, but for the kingdoms of "see me," "love me," "hold me," but "don't reveal me, where I am, because I am lost while I am helping you." Believe me, when I say this, you will blame everybody for castrating you when you really castrated yourself. I put myself in places that I knew would kill my love and passion and I did it anyways just to say, "somebody loves me."

Trusting Unlawful Soul Ties

There were many times that I would play for people that I knew did not like me but only needed my gift at the time. I knew that I was their last choice. "So what?" is what I said to myself. I will go and be a blessing to them and I did. I did so many things in the name of 'being a blessing' and this is not wrong when your motive is right, but the truth be told, it was because I was lost, and this is the way I chose to deal with it. No more soul ties in the name of 'being a blessing.' You may ask the question how all of this happened, well there was a principality in place. I have learned that it is the territory or jurisdiction of a prince, the country, that gives the *title* to a prince. The devil is the prince of the air (Ephesians 2:2). The word title = ownership, claim, right. It comprises all the elements constituting legal ownership - a legally just cause of exclusive possession. When the devil develops a principality in our minds or our bodies, he produces what is called a stronghold.

Stronghold mindsets are something that have a strong 'hold' on your mind. Because of strongholds, people are hurting all over the world. I grew up being pushed aside, cast off, and rejection was normal, acceptable. Then, I became an adult who had no direction in life, wondering aimlessly, bound, confused, and perplexed. I felt like I was being incarcerated mentally, physically, and spiritually but all the while laughing and smiling, most of time preaching God's Word. I was sentenced to a life sentence of emotional emasculation, depression, anxiety and low to no self-esteem. I was on a habitual death row of deadly desires - alcohol became a way of coping, and I began to engage in careless, unsafe, and uninhibited sexual activity.

Yes, I was one of these children who I was raised right, in church. I was being held captive behind these seemingly unsolvable bars and unavoidable walls, being made to believe that this was all there is to life. The real unsolvable and unavoidable walls were my own beliefs. Mentally messed up, emotionally emasculated, and spiritually lost, I was aimlessly wandering through life, bound, hopelessly waiting to die and imagining that everything will be over if I just cease from being. It was hard for me to see that life in God has a far more excellent and abundant life for me. I was struggling trying to break free, unable to come into the freedom that was promised to me. And finally, I came to understand that the price of my freedom has already been paid and all I have to do is COME.

'Broken' comes from the Hebrew word 'Shabar'. Shabar means 'to crush into pieces; shattered, bruised, violated; not functioning properly; disconnected; overwhelmed with sorrow; raped; plundered; maltreated and desecrated. The systems of the devil have emotionally emasculated the minds of people and placed them in a prison that they feel they will never be released from. They are being held captive and are in need of deliverance. This was my way of thinking *all the time*. Still, to this day I hear VOICES TELL ME that life is just a big circle.

There is an answer for the bound man or woman wandering through this life aimlessly. That is to repent (change the way we think) and be baptized (to be put into) into the name (the nature) of Jesus Christ (the original mind of Adam) and be filled with the Holy Ghost. We must know that looking into the face of God and asking Him to intercede finds true deliverance. The systems of the devil, who is a deceiver, use trickery to fight this battle of spiritual warfare. Because man is limited in his thinking, he often yields to the temptations of the systems and thus fails in the spiritual war.

THE MATRIX IS MORE THAN A MOVIE. The system understands that to gain control of the mind is to ultimately have control of the soul. This is how the devil caused the fall of man in the garden of Eden, because he deceived Eve into believing something that was not true. And when we believe what the enemy tells us, our belief just put us in *his* world. This was a deceptive measure that tricked the mind of Eve and placed a stronghold on her and because she was not awaked to spiritual warfare and the tricks of the devil, she yielded to the deception. Mind control is the nuclear weapon that the devil uses in spiritual warfare because of the destructive capabilities it has.

The Bible says in:

2 Corinthians 10:4-5

4. for the weapons of our warfare are not carnal but mighty through God to the pulling down of stronghold;
5. casting down imaginations, and every high thing that exalted itself against the knowledge of God, and bringing into captivity every thought to the obedience of Christ.

When the Bible says that our weapons are not carnal, this simply means that humanistic attempts are futile in spiritual warfare. We cannot defeat the devil with bombs and guns, but the weapons found in The Word of God will defeat the devil every time. Those weapons are mighty, through God, to the pulling down of strongholds.

Contrary to popular belief, alcohol, depression, narcotics, or elicit sexual activity is not what people are bound by - these are only the manifestations of the true bondage and that is the mind.

The Bible says in:

Proverbs 23:7

7. **For as he thinks in his heart, so is he.**

The devil knows that the way a person thinks is how that person will act. If he can convince a person to believe something that is not true, then he can cause them to fall and defeat them in this spiritual war. Therefore, the alcoholic thinks they need the alcohol in order to make it. They are bound because the devil has control of the mind. The drug addict thinks they can't survive without the drug and they are therefore, bound by drugs because the devil has control of the mind. The sex craved nymphomaniac thinks they will not survive without sex and therefore punishes their body because the devil has control of the mind. It's all bondage in the mind.

One of the main reasons why the church is not as successful as it could be in these areas is because we rather deal with the *fruit* of a thing than the *root* of it. All of the things that I just mentioned are all do to some sort of soul-tie or form of disconnection. When we disconnect from God, from our purpose, we will find ourselves in wrong places and with the wrong people. Without going to the root of things even our deliverance is delusional. Sometimes freedom is just another false perception.

CHAPTER 22

We Were Made for Life and Love

As much as I hated life and was hurt by love, the truth is I was made for life *and* love. Now this is a very hard thing to experience when life is stolen by the gift given to you. See, all I thought that I really knew how to do was play music and preach, anything outside of that was very hard for me. It was hard for me to fit in anywhere else. I was so caught up in preaching to the point that my childhood was robbed of great joy. I allowed my perception to rob me of living. I took my graduation picture sitting behind the desk acting like I was a Pastor in a 3-piece suit. And on top of all of that, I was preaching a revival on prom night.

The only time I was really happy was while *performing*. I didn't know how to laugh unless faking in while depressed which was one of my hiding places. I was about 30 years old before I owned my first pair of jeans and still it took a long time to be comfortable in them. All of my clothes were dark because I was taught that preachers didn't wear bright colors. Life and being happy was strange. I was 49 years old before I started to go on vacations, just to relax and not preach or play music. I knew the Bible verse that said God came to give us life and life more abundantly, but I did not know how to experience it.

Love was another thing that I struggled with because all of my dreams about love were always shattered. I had a love for my father and it's taken many years for me to understand his love and how *he* loved. My mother's love was great at times and then at others it was crazy. It took me many marriages and many trails to find out about the God Life and His unconditional love. Without the Holy Spirit in my life, my false perception would have kept me hidden from the life that was prepared for me. Being healthy and living life without regrets and shame seemed impossible. But God.

God began to show me that life was a gift from Him and that He is the substance of life and love. This began to change my mind about life and my chances of living and experiencing a God Life and His love. This belief woke something up in me, making me see life and love through His eyes and not my own. Now I live life in Him wherever I go, and I know love from both sides of the track, natural and spiritual. The life of Christ is also great outside of church or preaching. It took a long time for me to enjoy ice-cream, movies and fishing without thinking that I am displeasing God.

Change occurs because we understand the Divine Set-Up at a deep level and not to hinder this Divine Set Up because of pain or religious doctrine. I had to rise up in *consciousness* and learn that *change* is an aspect of love, which moves from the present understanding to that of a higher one. Just like plants naturally and instinctively move toward the sunlight, I was designed to move toward the light of love.

God, our *source* and *the truth* of our being, must be all things in all ways. And from this, in God's Time, our soul creates

Divine Order in a timely manner, based on our readiness to love and live. Our soul impeccably tailors itself to our awakening. When we move in trust and faith in this truth, we are able to constantly live in a state of grace, in gratitude for each sacred moment. Simply stated, we live the love we read about in His Word.

CHAPTER 23

Let Us Pass Over unto the Other Side

The things that I am about to say are not to overlook my sins (as I can't live in the guilt of sin since that's what God died for) but the pain that I caused and also the rejections that I received were for this reason alone - to learn and then *live*. We must come to a point where we allow rejection to be our motivation and not allow it to have us stuck at the starting line. Problems cannot be cemented but must be rivers that drive you to the next place.

God told me to not let anything in the middle make me fail to notice what is on the other side. Yes, I cried about my mistakes and yes, I had regrets, but God knew my weakness, my pride and my flesh – still He called me. This is why, when He was on the cross, He cried out, "Forgive them, for they know not what they do." We must still go to the *other side* of our problems and the *other side* of our pain.

Yes, I was wrong, but God is the only one that is right, and the truth is that God would rather *I be real first before trying to be right.* There comes a time when you make up your mind that your flesh will not stop you from doing your God-given assignment. "I will finish this" are the words of a warrior. I may be a Peter who denied Christ three times, but I will speak up at the day of

Pentecost. I may have doubted the resurrection like Thomas, but it has allowed me to see the nail prints in His hands. I may hit the rock like Moses in the wilderness and miss the promised land but later, I will be with Him on the Mount of Transfiguration. See, all these people (and many more) had their share of problems but, just like Paul, we must say, "I ran my race and finished my course."

Purpose can't stop because problems are there. It is *by* purpose that problems are discovered and solved. You must decide to explore, accept and understand how the purpose that God has given you works for and with you, because Godly spiritual growth is the understanding of yourself and your experiences. Remember, before you go up, you must go down. In all that you go through get wisdom for the next journey and then apply that knowledge. Keep in mind, the enemy will not wait for you to become a child of God and get all this wisdom in order for you to do God's Will, but the good part is that God uses the enemy to train you for the other side of your journey. When you get overcome, then you will be ready to be used. Moses was with Pharaoh for 40 years and then ran away only to be with God for 40 years before returning to lead the Israelites out of Egypt.

The enemy tried to destroy you, your potential, and power as a son of God, and he knows that your authority is over him. So, okay yes, he came at you when you were young, and yes, he came in your marriage and yes, he used all your family and friends to destroy you, *yet* you are still alive and with knowledge from the lessons about the enemy you overcame! You conquered some fears and you found out more about yourself in those places than you ever did before. Therefore, move on and transition to the other side of why these lessons were necessary.

John 21:15-17

¹⁵· So when they had dined, Jesus saith to Simon Peter, Simon, son of Jonas, lovest thou me more than these? He saith unto him, Yea, Lord; thou knowest that I love thee. He saith unto him, Feed my lambs.

¹⁶· He saith to him again the second time, Simon, son of Jonas, lovest thou me? He saith unto him, Yea, Lord; thou knowest that I love thee. He saith unto him, Feed my sheep.

¹⁷· He saith unto him the third time, Simon, son of Jonas, lovest thou me? Peter was grieved because he said unto him the third time, Lovest thou me? And he said unto him, Lord, thou knowest all things; thou knowest that I love thee. Jesus saith unto him, Feed my sheep.

After everything you did wrong, in the end, you will still hear the Lord saying the above instruction *"feed My sheep."* Regardless of how much we overcome there is an inward pull to conform, to govern our lives by the standards of our culture, but you must know what you're calling and purpose is on Earth and allow the lessons that you went through to get you to your God given purpose. So, when you lay your head to rest, you know that you did what was in you to do.

There is a great reason why God allows us to be in a wilderness before we get to our promised land. It's conversations that come up there in the wilderness that let you see *you*. Remember, that life is about freedom – the freedom which takes place among a people liberated from bondage. It is about equipping with the discipline and responsibility that comes with freedom. The discipline of freedom is not self-control; it's the ability to be and not judge or condemn; it's a place where we just observe. Freedom will be in contention with issues of survival. Survival is a trap to trueness, because in survival you can only handle the truth that's keep you alive, not truth that kills. This statement may not be easily understood but think about it and God will show you the revelation. Mere survival was in the wilderness, but *living* is what God has promised.

This is why many don't make it to the promised land because they never dealt with how they see themselves. A grasshopper complex will stop all the promises of God from flowing through you if you are not honest with yourself. When God talked about the promised land He says it's a land (which is a people) that flows with milk and honey. The key word there is '*flows.*' One of the things that God taught me was that there is no guarantee that when we train a person's mind, we train his heart. So, we trust *God* to change his heart while we renew his mind.

When we increase a person's knowledge of self (whose nature is evil), we can then increase their goodness (which is really not their own goodness, but God being demonstrated through them). Sometimes, only in extremity do we discover what to live by. You will need deliverance in order to go to your next level in God and in life.

What is Deliverance?

Deliverance comes from the Hebrew word 'Peleytah' or 'Peletah' (pronounced pel-ay-taw) which means "to set free", "to take and hand over to or leave for another", "to assist in giving birth: to aid in the birth of: to give birth to: to cause oneself to produce as if by giving birth", "to send something aimed or guided to an intended target or destination: to come through with."

Deliverance takes place in the spiritual realm, against principalities and powers, and spiritual wickedness in high places. Hence the battle for deliverance is not against flesh and blood. True deliverance comes by way of honesty and being willing to be naked and not ashamed. If we are not delivered in the spiritual world, then we are still bond in the physical world - whether we see it or not. It is important for every Christian to understand that the weapons of this battle are not carnal but mighty, through God, to the pulling down of strongholds. God ordains deliverance thus every believer should know, understand, and practice deliverance as an essential part of his/her walk with God. For indeed, "All have fallen short in the sight of God."

Shift or Satisfy the Old

When there is a call, there could also be a cry - a cry from the memory of the 'old man' (our old self) in leaving the things that I used to do. How do I betray the 'old man?' As sick as it looks right now, this man was my friend. these things were my life. But I must go, for I am in love now with the new: the health of my life and the health of my thoughts. I had been born for this moment, and I feel it, for it is so near. It's in my mouth, in my heart, and in my mind. I believe me, really for the first time, and I am ready to run like a fool but submit like a drowning man to life. So, I shift and no longer satisfy the 'old man.' Yes, I feel his pain, but I must go. I may miss him, but I must move on!

Understanding Both Sides

We all must learn how to live with ourselves. That's the good and the so-called 'bad.' We must understand our Cain and Abel, Simon and Peter; knowing Jesus the Christ, humanity and divinity.

I had to learn that just because I was chosen, does not mean that I can't be confused. I had to face the battle in my mind that said to me "how can I help others, yet at the same time need help myself?" This can cause such a battle to the point that you may remain stuck in one place. How long do we battle before we walk into our destiny? How important is it to learn what I need to in order to come out? The prodigal son had to come to himself in order to return home to his father the right way. When you come to understand the journey as well as the destination, it can bring you to a healthy place. The Bible says, in Romans 8:28, that "all things work together for the good." The hard part is accepting that *all things* are working toward something good in your life.

It has taken me years to accept this principle and to see how bad things can get in order to help me or bring me to a better place. All throughout the Bible you see this war we all face; our will fighting against our God ordained destiny. It takes years, for many, to understand what is happening and the choosing of which son, Will or Destiny, who will lead. Only through honesty and true self-evaluation can transitioning from this war take place.

CHAPTER 24

Known in the Flesh, Overlooked in the Spirit

> "And they were offended in him But Jesus said unto them, a prophet is not without honor, save in his own country, and in his own house." Mark 6:4

My elementary and junior high school friends know me as 'Duvall', or 'the drummer that plays in church.' My high school friends know me as Robert. In church I was called 'The Preacher.' My behavior, in the flesh, was a road block for many, but I had to know that regardless of how much I fell, I was still God's Man. Just like David, Moses, Paul and anyone else that God has decided to use, problems of the flesh comes with purpose in the spirit.

One of the real problems with being called is not always how people see and forgive you but seeing in yourself what God still sees. People will judge you when they know something about your past or your flesh. Some people will not hear you, but that can't be your conviction. True conviction must come from the Lord, not people's opinion. This is the main reason why preachers that are from out of town can come to your church and say the same things that you, as the home pastor, have been saying for years and people act like it's a word straight out of God's Mouth. People want 'clean' vessels to hear from, not 'dirty' ones. The issue with this thinking is that *the only clean vessel is Jesus*. The problem is that the less people know about you the better they feel, which either will make you lie about your problems or hide them, so you can be heard. This mindset has helped you to be fake, or it created a falsehood that God can only use 'clean' people.

Trust when I say this, the first time your members, friends, or followers find out the truth about you, they may leave the church, stop the phone calls, and you will be hurt. You will be at fault for trying to control things through lies. If they refuse to hear God because of your past, then they may also refuse to be used by God because of *their* past. This is not your problem, it's a lack of understanding of God's Love.

Dealing with Me: Emotion from the Mind

Our emotions are very important to the move of the spirit because this is the place where we feel. It's also the place where we are convinced that things in the earth realm are real. We can be in a movie and start crying actual tears while all the time we know that they are acting but our emotions feel what we are looking at and release tears. If our emotions can release real tears from non-real moments, what else can they tell us that is not real?

The flesh plays on our emotions, to get us out of the spirit and deeper into it. This is what the flesh tries to do often because these feelings help us become mad and then respond out of our emotions and *not* by the spirit. If we are led by our emotions, we may never be led by God's Spirit. But we also can't deny our emotions either. The Bible says to be angry, but sin not. Our emotions are needed to reveal where we are but not what we should do.

Intellect from the Mind

The intellect is very dangerous because we need to use the knowledge of God, not our knowledge, neither that of man. When we think that we are smart enough, then we start to think that there is no need for God. Or we tell God, "thanks for the help, but I will take the wheel from here."

The Mystery of the Mess

You were emptied out so that you could be filled with Him. This is the reason why so many things in your life were allowed. I have said so many times God, "why did you allow this?" or "God why didn't you stop that?" Yet, what I say now is "thanks for it all because those painful things assisted me in knowing myself like nothing else could." I am happier now than I've ever been. I am more complete, more fulfilled. All because of the emptying out of things that I thought I needed and wanted to happen. This journey brought me to my purpose. It was my pain that was calling me to my purpose. It was my pain that was teaching me about my purpose and now I've got it. It was never actually a 'problem' but my 'purpose' that was placed from the beginning of my life. It was telling me how these problems I was dealing with is the reason why I am here. I'd learned what I was void of was my ministry. These problems were not for me but to enable me to relate to others. Wow, I am okay, I am not cursed, not a failure. I was being trained! Lol (laugh out loud) wow, wow, wow, finally I know why all of that happened!

There is a smile on my face. I came to realize this about my life - all the time I did have purpose and was being trained for it from the day I was born. God was using the 'void' to create the appetite and it worked because I am hungry for my purpose. I do not preach to get fulfillment but rather helping others brings fulfillment to me. God is the best chess player in the world! He knows that character is formed in community, but it is tested in isolation. Most of the time it's the alone place that leads to self-discovery. There are two 'problem' places that will reveal you the world:

1. This is my beloved Son (Jesus)
2. The wilderness (being tempted of the devil)

Burdened Down Until I Can't Look Up (So Help Me God)

There were so many days that I just wanted to give up, this flesh thing is too much! I was tired of masturbating while studying God's Word. I began to say, "I am a fake and a user of the Spirit. A Jim Jones." I was in the struggle between 'I, who loved God' and 'me, who no good thing dwells in.' This struggle was driving me crazy! It was a burden to be called and confused. I was tired of hiding but telling the truth. It made people question my calling. I can't help that God will not stop talking to me because of my issues.

Yes, I know that God hates divorce, but He also hates how I lie and hide because that's what church people would rather hear. If I marry the woman because I don't want to stop having sex with her, it's okay. But if I leave because she stops having sex with me then I'm wrong. Well, the truth is, my foundation for marrying her was just as wrong. And I know that it is better to marry than to burn, but most of the time, after you get married you still end up burning up from passion anyways, and then you may find yourself cheating. Let's just start being honest and look for real answers to these problems and not fig leaves to cover up with. When Apostle Paul talks about the war from within, this is so real. Also, Jesus talks about the weeds and the tares growing together but when we see this in people, we act like they are so wrong, but the truth is that it's in all of us.

We must be willing, every morning, to face ourselves in the spirit just like we do in the natural - seeing the purpose, passion, and power that is in us. If we say that we wish to see someone 'face to face,' we may mean that we desire to have a meeting with that person. The first person you need to meet is *you*. Your stubbornness is hurting you and stopping you from meeting the God in you.

How can you love others, when your love is in captivity to a false belief? How can you help others when your helpmate's soul is lost and has not been found (renewed)? When you get up in the morning you must look at *you* in order to clean *you*, and to dress *you*. If you read the manual (the Bible), stubbornness was not part of the Plan or in the Design, but troubleshooting is in the manual to help you to deal with non-designed problems. Have you spoken openly to yourself about this virus that is in your system of thinking?

Most of my life, I was thinking that I needed people to help me and support me, but the truth was that I needed to help myself be honest with my weakness. I needed to know that, regardless of how anointed I thought I was, I was still no better than the next person. Yes, I was raised up in the church, but I was as lost as the next person in the world. As I look back over things and see the many times God made a way for me to escape, still, I returned back to the same things that I said were killing me; back to the same people that I said meant me no good. Well, I know that it is a snake, but I was still trying to make it a friend. Maybe in the mind of the snake he is thinking that I am trying to hurt him, since I am in his area, and in his space, so he bit me out of fear and out of his nature. He followed his nature, but I am mad because I ignored mine and got bit because of it. Now, who really has the problem, me or the snake?

When the Blind Man Can See the Man in the Mirror

As I've pondered over this statement (which I have heard for many years) I ask, "how do we do that?" and "why do we need to?" Are we victims of the self-image that has lied to us and has made us believed that what we see is who we really are? Wow!

Then, we are a mess if the outside of us determines the value and quality of our life. We are no more than skin and tissue, clothes that we either bought or borrowed to fit into the make-believe world. Can we really stand in front of a man-made mirror and see a God being? What mirror can we look at to see if we are loving or beautiful? And if we do this, are we lying to ourselves or are we allowing the mirror to be God?

Let's just tell the truth: we, as a people, must stop allowing things and people from the outside to judge our value and the likeness of who we are. I am great because of who my Father is, and it is His quality that I possess. When I use Him as my mirror, then the truth is really told. When was the last time you looked at God from a pure place and when you saw Him, you said "that's me?"

1 John 3:2-3

2 beloved, now we are the children of God, and it has not yet been revealed what we shall be, but we know that when is He revealed, we shall be like Him, for we shall see Him as He is,

3. and everyone who has this hope in Him purifies himself, just as He is pure.

Do you see a man in the mirror or do you see God in a man? When I look in the mirror and see a man I begin to blame, but when I look in the mirror and see God in a man, I listen. One of the most important aspects of the truth is training the eyes to see. Stop trying to *set* things right but begin to *see* things right. Remember, perception is everything. What you are seeking and searching for has always been with you. You just need to see it.

New Laws of Thoughts About Me

If God has a plan for my life, then I must start on the journey and not stop until I reach the place for which I was created to occupy. I must say to myself, "nothing and no one will hinder me from my destiny!" I can't accept just being happy, I must search for and reach for fulfillment. Fulfillment comes by having a clear sense of personal identity.

One of the biggest lessons in life, for me, was to not allow anything or anyone to define me outside of God. This means no title in the church or in the world, no designer clothes or anything... and my greatest deliverance was being delivered from people's opinion. There was a time in my life that if you were mad at me it would root up my very being because I didn't want to not be loved. I was addicted to praise and approval. I needed people to say good things about me in order to feel good about me myself. And when you let things and people define you, this will be your fight for the rest of your life.

I worked at a bank and one of the things that I have learned is that a lot of people spend plenty of money to keep away identity thieves. But what if you are the one giving your identity away? It was so surprising, and hurtful at the same time, when I realized that I was allowing myself to be abused or robbed out of the treasure that was in me - just to have a hug, or to hear people say I belong. One of the greatest tricks of the devil is to have us not value life and the meaning behind it. It's hard to see its meaning when you have already devalued it by saying things like, "no one will miss me," or "I have no purpose."

When I think of purpose I think of the original intent of a thing in the mind of its owner. What is God's Purpose for your life and are you living that purpose now? What is your mission in life? Without searching for your purpose, you can become a slave to all things. This is why vision is so important because you can never have life where there is no vision. And all visions should be written down and viewed every day. It's sad to say but we, as people, have too much to live with and too little to die for. When your vision, that was sent by God, becomes so important to the point that you give your life and time to it, then it will come to pass.

Please Don't Let One Thing Kill Everything

If the devil could, he would take just one wrong thing in your life and try to kill everything else, because of your position in God. Sometimes, this mentality is not from the devil but us. We let one main thing in our life make us believe that *everything* is over, and we are done. We give power to a problem when we believe in the problem and not in what God has said about it. Sometimes, we let our need to be loved be the killer of all relationships in our life. Please don't see love as an enemy.

The enemy is always trying to have you look at things based upon past failures. What this does is keep you at the same level and you never learn from what you just went through. The one thing that keeps coming back up again is the one thing that can teach you the greater lessons, if you step back and look at what's going on.

CHAPTER 25

God Hears You, Too

In Genesis 20:9-12 it talks about how Abraham has two sons, Ishmael and Isaac. Ishmael's name means 'God hears (God will hear).' I love the Bible for the truth that it reveals - that even a child of the flesh, God will still hear. The other son was named Isaac and his name means 'to laugh.' Amazingly, the child of the flesh's name, Ishmael, (which means God will hear) and the child of the promise, Isaac, (which means God will laugh or God has smiled).

How many of us, as the children of Ishmael, have been told that God does not hear us? But the Bible shows us here that the very name means that God has a plan even for those that were born of the flesh. This is the child that was called the crack baby, or the child of a prostitute or the child without a father in their life. I write to tell you that God hears you and that He loves you too. Many people made me feel like God would not hear me or use me because of problems in my life. My last name is 'Jenkins' and some people would call me 'Jenkie Jenks' referring to me as a jinx (bad luck). This made me feel like I was cursed or that I have a curse on me just by my last name. Then I would hear people say, "God don't hear sinners" and I was a big one so "God doesn't hear me?" But, all these things were lies and the truth is that God heard me just like He heard the prayers of the children of Israel even though they prayed for over 400 years before Moses came to help, but God still heard them.

The devil can bring you into so much guilt and shame because of your decisions. Many things like abortion, murder, and rape can cause you to believe that God doesn't hear you. In the book of Genesis, it talks about how Cain killed his brother Abel. God heard the cry of Abel's blood coming from the ground. If God can hear a dead man's blood from the ground, be clear that God hears us regardless of *where* we are in life.

The danger with thinking that God doesn't hear us from where we are, may cause us to ignore the warning signs and never begin to have God fix the problems. Our main concern is to be whole and not just survive. God allows our flesh to be seen so that we can be honest about what's in our mind and to begin to talk to Him about these things.

We are *all* cracked vessels being used in the hands of The Master. God is working on *all* of us, because our lives are an answer to a problem. After God allows a man to hurt deeply, it is then, that He uses a man greatly. This is a very hard lesson and most of us will leave the class before the healing begins. So that later (could be weeks, months, or years), we find ourselves back in the class of life again. We must endure the night in order to enjoy the morning.

The miracle is when you see the answer in the problem. The enemy hopes that you see the problem as *you* and not see you as *the answer*. Please don't miss your appointment with a miracle by running from the problem. Remember that God not only hears you, but He sees *you* as you are, too.

You can't repair the broken places, if you don't expose where they are. The devil is after the *place*, not just the broken pieces.

Ephesians 4:26-27

26. be ye angry and sin not; let not the sun go down upon your wrath;

27. neither give place to the devil.

The Bible here talks about being angry, but not sinning. Most false perceptions hide in lies and false smiles. Being angry is a real emotion that allows your feelings to be free. Without this real expression you could still be in a false place thinking that you are okay. I have to tell the truth, even about my emotions and how life has made me feel. I couldn't even begin to practice forgiveness until I got mad in my emotions about what I thought was done to me. Many days, I went through life laughing and smiling, but at the same time, God was hearing my cry for help and the cry of "why is this happening to me?"

CHAPTER 26

Being Centered, Being True, and Being Real

Sometimes, we want God to move fast in our life. Understanding that we lack patience is often very hard to accept. The real problem is in not knowing how to focus because without focus, many thoughts will come in and move you all over the place. Focus determines mastery, and anything that has the ability to keep your attention *may* have mastered you.

Who are the roommates in your mind, to the point that whenever you are bored, what strongholds come out of those rooms in your mind? You have to learn that your focus determines your energy and where there is no focus, then your energy lays dormant. Also, when there is no focus, your senses go wild! You start looking everywhere and at everyone. You may cheat in your mind with so many people and they never know it. **Sight affects desire.**

What you keep looking upon, you will eventually pursue. You can ask lots of people from the Bible about this one. Just ask David about when he was on the rooftop, looking down and seeing another man's wife - this was the beginning of a great fall.

I had to learn how not to be led by my eyes, my flesh, and my emotions. Being centered, true, real with myself was hard, at first, because I didn't know what it looked like. Growing up with so much drama and confusion (which became my norm), God had to teach me the value of balance. My family life lies as a way of life and this shaped my perception of love, peace, and so many other things. Even though this was crazy, it also created a hunger for real talk and real people. Only by God's Truth, was balance received in my life. Once I tasted it, nothing else mattered.

    My relatives and my church family hated that I came to this truth, because it made me transparent and I would tell it all. I didn't care who knew because I needed to be truthful in order to be free. My health was dependent upon me being truthful in order to be centered. I was determined to not fall down, all emotional, every time something didn't go my way. Truth became the foundation on which I chose to stand. Then, I became healthy without the need of others making me *feel* healthy. I no longer was dependent on the approval of others. I was delivered from people's opinion of me when I began sharing my pain and testimony. It felt so good to be real and balanced with the power from God to stand as a healthy man. I can stand in the mirror and see a man of God, not perfect but free.

CHAPTER 27

Add it All Up

We are the sum total of what we have learned from all who have taught us, both great and small. This is so major in your life because you may not even know how many classes you have been in and how much you have learned from people, bad and good. Everything in life is a part of God's Plan and as you grow, you will begin to see how it all adds up. Life is like a 100-piece puzzle - every piece is a part to the picture and every piece has its place. Every piece has been cut to connect to the next piece. The more you release your false perception, it all begins to make sense. Releasing false perception is not about removing what you experience but it's about putting the pieces in their right place. Only by the truth will the picture of your life add up.

Don't overlook anything and I mean, nothing! Your birth pains and struggles one day will add up. Those answers to questions about those hard days will begin to have great meaning. The days when you thought that God had left you and you were so lost, will become testimony.

When I think back on my family, music, preaching, and the entire ups and downs that came with these things, I understand that those were pieces to the puzzle of my life. I now can say, with a smile on my face, "thank you Lord." I used to say, "why me

God?" but now I do understand. It's a beautiful thing when it all starts to add up. I understand, now, the strict training and why God couldn't make it easy on me. It's like going to college to be a doctor but some of the classes that are required seem to have nothing to do with being a doctor. But, later in life, you see that those classes were not only about being a doctor but also about being a citizen.

    Things will begin to add up regarding the Kingdom and where and how you fit in. Your purpose and passion will begin to breathe.

CHAPTER 28

Nakedness Is the Dress for Glory

If you really want to be free, then *un*dress. Take off all the clothes of your reality and look at the mirror and tell me what you see. When Adam and Eve were in the garden, they were naked and not ashamed, and the real reason is because the glory of God was their covering. When they made figs leaves to hide themselves, it demonstrated that this mindset came from their fall. This was the beginning of a man-made covering, because clothes are not what they lost, they had lost God's Glory.

The glory of God comes to allow you to be naked and not ashamed of where you are or what you did or had been. I have noticed that the most anointed people are those who have the worst lives but are honest about where they are. Where there is nakedness and honesty, God's Glory will dwell. How can David be a man after God's Heart with the kinds of sin he committed? Maybe, because of his honesty, like saying to God that he was born in sin and shaded in iniquity. Saying things like "Lord, give me a right spirit and a clean heart," brings the glory. David was not just honest about his sin, but he was honest about his enemy, which is why he could ask God to kill his enemies. Because **the glory of God** rested on him.

God knows your weaknesses, so why lie and hide at the expense of losing His glory? Being naked is a wonderful thing because it removes the burden of trying to pretend. I was carrying so much shame and guilt, which was never God's Doing. God wanted me to know, in all things, that I could be real and true. God's Love covers a multitude of faults. His love is why glory is present. Don't worry, you can be covered so come just as and wherever you are.

CHAPTER 29

Honesty Will Cause You to See God

Psalm 40:8

8. I delight to do thy will, O my God: yea, thy law is within my heart.

These were my words as well, because my heart was after God in one way while in another, my heart was so far from Him. The questions that you should ask yourself in your struggles are:
1. Where am I?
2. How am I living?
3. What do I believe?

It's the flesh that must summit to God, not the born-again seed. Being honest about this place takes time and this will, also, bring you to a place of maturity. Many times, because of your struggles, you can become double-minded. It's just like the man in the Bible that says, "Lord help me with my unbelief, not the part that believes." These kinds of struggles will bring you to a better understanding of God's love and a deeper relationship with The Father.

Psalm 40:9

⁹· I have preached righteousness in the great congregation: lo, I have not refrained my lips, O Lord, thou know.

This was my excuse when I thought that God was mad at me or when my conviction became hard to ignore. I would tell God of all that I do for Him and how, regardless of my life, that I always tell people the truth about Him. But, after all that preaching, I was still living a lie, living in bondages. This is very common with people in leadership. We hide behind what we *do* and not *how* we live and think, in private.

Psalm 40:10-13

¹⁰· I have not hid thy righteousness within my heart; I have declared thy faithfulness and thy salvation: I have not concealed thy loving kindness and thy truth from the great congregation.

¹¹· Withhold not thou thy tender mercies from me, O Lord: let thy loving kindness and thy truth continually preserve me.

¹²· For innumerable evils have compassed me about: mine iniquities have taken hold upon me, so that I am not able

to look up; they are more than the hairs of mine head: therefore, my heart failed me.

Verse 12 is where truth now speaks from the human side.

¹³· Be pleased, O Lord, to deliver me: O Lord, make haste to help me.

You see how it took some verses to get to the truth of how the heart was really feeling? This is you and I and, in many cases, this is the false perception that we live. Without real honesty you can't get real help. Only truth from God can really set us free.

There was a girl that had gotten raped by a man, but when they investigated, it started to look like the girl was not really raped but had consented. But the main reason why she was declared raped was because the man heard and confessed that she cried for help. Honesty brings us to a place where we admit that we need help. This is the best cry in the world.

Peter was drowning after following the Word of God but in his trouble, he cried for help. We must be honest in our need for deliverance as well as in our need to be used. We can't keep using God's grace when we don't really cry out for change. Where sin abounds, grace does much more abound but remember we still can frustrate grace and be turned over to a reprobate mind. Let's learn to be honest about it *all*. When was the last time you really cried for help? Are you seeking help in the place where you are being raped or in the place where you know that you are drowning? Let's not just cry for help to get out but cry for help to never go back, to move forward.

CHAPTER 30

Healing the Family from the Beginning

The Good News is That the Bad News is Wrong Family

Sex does not create babies, God does. The Bible says in Psalm 127:3 "Lo, children *are* a heritage of the Lord: *and* the fruit of the womb *is his* reward." So, this means that our parents didn't bring us here, God did. Then, there must be a purpose to every child's life. It took me years to believe that I was not a mistake and that I had a real purpose in life that didn't always mean pain or rejection. Most of us can't love what we didn't plan or can't control.

It also didn't help knowing that my mother had said things, while I was in the womb, which may have given me this feeling, by vibration alone, that I was in the way of her life or just not wanted at the time. She would say things like, "if this baby was not here then I could go out," or "this boy is too big, and I can't afford any more clothes." These stories that were told to me, just pushed me to believe I was in the way, that I had no real place here. These words became my words for years.

I lost some great people in my life because I made them responsible for the things that I could not deal with or the things that I hid for years. Especially when they gained my trust, then I would download on them all those years of pain and stress, in turn stressing them to see me like this. It was too much for them.

I didn't believe that I was the next move in God, or the next blessing in my family. No, I believed that I was a curse, and I would say to myself, "that's why my name is Jenkins. That's why people used to call me the 'Jenkster'" and I believed that I was a jinx.

We are told that the devil is a liar, but we still believe what he says. All that I have been through was really good news. It was really saying that I had purpose and that God's hands were on me. But I lied to myself about the good news because bad news kept me safe in my perception and not in God's truth.

My mother may not have known, from the beginning, the responsibility of the child in her belly, the child of her future, the child from Heaven but God did. See, children can never be an accident, so purpose must be discovered. I say to all families that were chosen to carry the gift, please no more abortions, in or out of the womb. This message is not just about human babies, but also spiritual babies that are in the womb of our spirit and mind. Stop aborting your dreams, desires, or your calling. Stop going to the doctor of doubt, fear, and disbelief. Trust The Father for it *all* and let's stop lying about the good news.

When we are pregnant, we can't go everywhere because of the baby. You must, also, watch what you eat. This is so true in the spiritual realm as well. Watch the words that go into our spirit, for the baby needs to be around love, peace, and unity. You are favored because of what's *in* you. The real gift is life, freedom, and most of all love. Please, in all of your understanding get understanding!

CHAPTER 31

Living a Life of Legacy

To me, the legacy that we can leave behind is a life that exemplified Christ – willing to suffer in the name of love and show the world that to be in God is the best place to be. There is the need, in all of us, to find a sustainable and dependable "other than self-reliance" or to offer oneself to something beyond our own being. Something that is regarded as supremely worthy of our life's ultimate devotion, for empowerment against life's crippling crisis.

The Marriage of Legacy:
Vision and Legacy Must go Together

How far do you see yourself going? Have you allowed the circumstances of life to rob you of vision? I believe that until we complete things that God has put in us, even death can't stop us. Legacy is what we leave behind but vision is what we see before dying. When we understand this concept, then we will begin to "work" the journey in the middle. I am writing this book because I am leaving a legacy of victory, never having allowed the wrong set of "eyes" to tell my story.

Vision is Rallying People to a Better Future

When you really believe in what you see, you will also know that visions never have only one person in it. The puzzle is *one picture,* but *many pieces.* True vision brings us all in the picture. Vision says, "I see it, so I know that we can do it." Vision tells us to hold on because the vision must come to pass. The more vision you have, the more meaning life has to you.

Vision is Calling the Invisible into Visibility

Vision is what causes the prodigal son's father to be outside waiting until he comes walking home. Visions speak to a dead man called Lazarus until he comes walking out of a tomb. Vision becomes the will power to get away from false perceptions and move into the real, God-intended plan for our lives.

Vision is Usually Determined by Your Burden and Your Faith

We are not called to be successful. We are called to be faithful. When we are faithful, success, by the Master's standards, will be achieved.

CHAPTER 32

Joy and Pain During the Journey

When I was about six years old, I'd walk to school. It was about one and half miles from the house. That was when I discover, in my spirit, that I was gifted. Searching for love, I would write a song while walking every day. I was so excited to the point that I could not wait to close that front door when I got back home later that day and begin making up songs to God. It was my greatest joy to bring this gift out. I was six years old writing songs from my heart and crying all the way to school.

See, I didn't really find God in a church or from going to a revival. He was in my heart as a little boy. Through my musical gifts, as a child, I knew the presence of God from singing. And as I would sing, I could feel the chills on my face. Music, singing, and writing were the first things that made me aware of love. It wasn't my love for my father or my mother, but for me, love introduced itself by way of music. That is how I came to know love.

Now that I think about it, what was really going on from the inside of me at age of six is that I could write a song. Not something that I heard on the radio but a song that I made up to express my love and pain, at six years old. I, now, realize that my pain was doing the writing, my pain was calling and saying *express.* The first song that I played on the piano was a song I wrote. Some people drink to express, others fight, but for me, I used my musical gifts and my love for God as my hiding place. No one would expose me there because it looked like the right thing to do. And because it blessed so many people, who would know that under all those songs and messages, I was hurting and wanted to die?

I hated myself because of how I saw the real me – life based on need. As my needs became greater so did my gift and this is when the war began. As I got older, I started playing music for a lot of 'stars' in the gospel world and people began to say to me, "your gift has made *room* for you." That's a Bible verse that people love to say when you begin to be so-called famous or exposed in the world. I hated to hear that, because I went in those rooms with a gift. I came out with much more.

The things that I saw and was touch by did so much more damage to me, to the point that sometimes I wish I was never gifted. The truth about those *rooms* is that, it's not about you. it's about your *gift*. People will use you because of your gift. The most abused gift is the gift of love. I saw little gifted boys go in those rooms and come out as little gifted girls. I saw honest people go in those rooms and come out as liars. Those rooms will bring out what's in you or expose your weakness and your real motive.

We don't hear about the rooms that your gift takes you in, but never lets you out of. Many times, the real you will leave with them and not with you! My gift was being praised. while my character was being raped and abused. See, these gifts can cause you to sell your soul to be praised, and to hide the real insecurity that you carry.

The power of rape is that its makes you work so very hard to try to get back the person that was stolen. See, if your house gets broken into and some valuable things are stolen, you may be able to replace them and sometimes even get something better. But, sometimes, you can never get back what those particular things meant to you. Well the truth is that those were things. When you are raped, you are not just violated, you are robbed. When that person gets up and looks at you with the expression that says, "you will never be the same," or that look which says, "yes, I just overpowered you and took what I wanted", that also says "you are weak and always will be" - especially when it's someone that you know or that you loved and trusted - how do you react?

See, many people may never say this, but this is one of the main reasons why so many men in the church are just acting like dogs in heat. They think they need so much sex because they are really trying to get back that which was stolen. If you've never been there or don't understand, then it makes it easy to say, "get over it," or to "why does he need to be praised so much?"

I saw more homosexuals and lesbians in the gospel arena then I ever saw in the world. I saw preacher's wives with other women. I knew women that were sleeping with the husband and his wife and the husband didn't even know that the wife was going both ways. When I was traveling on tour, many times, they would come to the dressing room right before going on stage and ask us questions like, "who want some weed/drugs/ men or women?" To me this was the Tree of Knowledge of Good and Evil.

There are many things that God allows, and you must ask the question 'why?' If you don't know the darkness of your gift, you may never use it in the light. Remember, being a light is not only a gift but also a burden. It's things like this that really give you a false perception of life. The purpose of teaching a lesson is for the student to pass the test. Everything in life is a class, a lesson and a test.

CHAPTER 33

Identities Stolen

The first security of the spirit is to protect you from *you*. The mind of the slave will fight the mind of a free man. Your flesh is the slave and your spirit is the free man. Expect the fight. The slave hates this place of freedom. He says to the free man, "you think too much, and you think you know it all." He says "why do you question everything?" and "don't go so deep." There is a slave you and a free you but most of us allow the slave us to rule the free us. But our real identity is in the free side of who we truly are.

I discovered another gift at a very early age. I could quote five to six chapters of the Bible when I was about eight years old. I was the Adult Sunday School teacher at 12, but as the revelation of God's Word grew in me so did the rejection. Because I was gifted, I was also hated -that's what my mind told me and that's what rejection will tell you. The voice of pain, sometimes, is the god we call "lord." Just as God uses trouble to reveal who we are, remember, the devil uses trouble to *hide* who we are or uses trouble to *define* us.

I lost my first identity in a lie that I believed from people. It was about love that my mother didn't have for me. That was not true, but I believe it. Why it is so easy to believe some lies about ourselves? Maybe it's somethings we just want to believe. It's less work to believe a lie than to reveal a truth.

The second loss of identity was in my father, because he did love me - given what love he had and his understanding of love. I came to learn, later, that his childhood life was bad also. Still, I was so into myself that I didn't let his story have any weight in my life. **Remember that pain is selfish.**

See, after many years my mother did marry again, but this guy struggled with homosexuality and now I was being hunted by my demons. People would ask how I'd learn to be a man, when my example is from one who does not want to be a man? But his love was more like God's than the man I wanted to be like, which was my natural father. My stepfather was also tall and very handsome and could play the piano extremely well. I had a baby grand piano in my living room at the age of 12, and a B3 1000 organ with a Leslie speaker (one of the old ones with the tube in it), which sounded great.

My stepfather was the only father that most of my friends knew and everybody loved him. He was a very nice man but just had many problems, and I saw them. It takes a mature person to know the struggle of their heroes and still give them their respect. It was nothing for me to come into the bathroom and see eyelashes on the sink that were not my mother's but my stepfather's. Many times, he would dye his hair red, green, and gray. But this was the same man that would take me everywhere with him to play the drums because he played the piano. So, that gave me a chance to express myself. He also believed in me being called as a young preacher.

When he went to audition for a church, he would tell the Pastor that if his son couldn't play drums there, then neither would he play the piano. I loved this man. He cared for me, looked out for me, but he was gay. My mother married a gay man. Wow! I loved my mother and knew that she wanted to be loved, but could a man, who was gay, love her? Can a gay man love me? Well, my natural father, who was a playboy, didn't show me love, but this man loved me, and he understood my gift. He took out time to be with me. Well, am I gay? This was the question that I would ask myself, from time to time.

My father in ministry, that licensed me, was his bubby (close friend) and he was called to preach as a child, like I was. So, he took me in, but he also struggled with homosexuality. I could not get away from perverted love - it was all around me, and it was from people that befriended me and gave me real love.

I remember my stepfather's friend, who was staying with us in our basement. He was 'Michael' by day and 'Michele' by night. One day, when I was in school coming out of class after hearing the bell ring (I was in junior high and all the kids ran out of class), I looked up and saw Michele (oh, I mean Michael), dressed in full drag, hollering my name. He told me that he'd lost his key and wanted to use mine to get into the house. Remember now, he sounded just like a woman and he looked like a woman, but everybody knew he was a man. My feelings were so hurt because my mother let this guy come up to my school. All of my friends saw him/her and they now knew that a gay guy stayed with us.

This was another thing that made me very concerned about my manhood, so I declared in my mind that I would sleep with as many women as I could to make sure that I was not gay. I would be a playboy, like my real father before I'd be gay - without even knowing that I was hiding my false identity by having sex. Sex became my identity for manhood since I could not find a man in my life that was not gay and who understood my gift and calling. Most of the people I know who can understand my pain and shame, my calling and anointing, are the ones who have sexual problems as well. This is a very common problem among musicians and entertainers. What do you do when your identity is stolen by your gift? What do you do when a problem knows you and can identify with you, better than a promise can?

When identity is stolen, purpose is also lost, which means happiness is not coming from within. Happiness is possible only when one is busy doing his purpose. The body must toil, the mind must be occupied, and the heart must be satisfied. But this mindset comes from knowing who you really are. We must be searching for a clearer sense of identity and purpose, which brings better relationships, and more balanced living.

Identity Saved by Friends

People are placed in our lives to help us wake up. Well, in my growing up years from six to 12, I had some friends. Person One was a friend who lived around the corner and who all the girls liked. I was the running nose boy that didn't have girls yet, even though we were too young anyway, but this guy received me as his friend. He didn't play drums, was not even a musician, but he was my friend. He was there to wake me up. He was there for years later when I would get lost in what real friendship was. But because of this friend, I could look back and see the truth that real friends don't need you to be them *or* them to be you. They just need for *you* to be you. This friend never judged me or made me feel less than.

He was a very handsome young man and people liked him very much. I was ignored, but not by him. We are friends even to this day and we can go years without talking and when I call him, we pick up where we left off, like there was never any space between us. He taught me what a friend looks like, without a need. And this kind of space was valuable in my mind.

I realized that he was put in my life as a wakeup call. Everything in our lives is a wakeup call - from who your father and mother are, to where you were born, to who you live by and grew up with. Everything and I mean everything, is a wakeup call, if you are listening. We must always remember that when God speaks to us He also speaks to others about us. Everybody needs a friend in their life, like John the Baptist in the Bible was to Jesus; Peter was a friend to James and John; Paul and Silas were friends and many others. We all need a friend who can witness the greatest in us. How can you call him or her your best friend if they cannot witness the goodness in you? One of the purposes of having friends is for them to keep you being real with yourself.

Do you have any friends in your life who think and will say that you are yielding yourself to greatness and that your time and your turn has come? If not, question that friendship. True friends are willing to draw you out. They will take time with you and believe in you; they will give you a chance to spread your wings and lift you up; smile at you when times are at their worst.

Friends Are Those Persons That Will Not Forget or Let You Forget What They Saw in You

Person Two was another friend who struggled with his family, so we had common problems that enhanced our friendship. When you are young, most of the time, its common problems that really bring you together. He was always at my house eating because his family was so big that when he came home too late all of the food would be gone. So, he ate with us most of the time.

We had so much in common: we both loved to play cards and loved women. Our birthdays were three days apart. But we were, also, great sinners together. This person was a real friend and we could talk about how we wished that our fathers were around. This friend had only seen his father twice in his whole life. That became our strength, because in our minds, we were all that the other had.

We were drinking buddies, and we did everything together. He was one of the friends that, when you see me, you knew that he was somewhere in the room. He never judged me as well, but he watched me change and, later on in life, we both changed for the better. But he was the one who revealed to me that when I became a preacher, it was then that I lost my identity. It was him who could tell me the truth about myself and I knew that it was truth because we have been through too much for me to question his motives. He brought my mind back to a reality that 'Robert' should always be 'Robert' regardless of the position that he may play in my life. Real friends will not let you lie to yourself.

Remember in the Bible when Peter told Christ that he would follow Him no matter what, but then Christ had to be a real friend and say to Peter, "you are lying again. Not only will you not follow me, but you will deny me, and that's okay for now." But later on, when you're mature, go and strengthen your brothers. Real friends don't have to lie to you because they know that your friendship can handle the truth!

Person Three was a friend I grew up with and was a preacher as a young man as well. We went to school together and we worked at the same place, had some of the same struggles. His father was not in his life and it was hard for him growing up. The area where he was a great friend in my life was in the area of confidence - he had it and he knew that I did not.

    He would always tell me that I didn't know my worth and how I would settle for less rather than the best. He was that friend who understood me and never allowed me to be nothing other then what I was at the time, but he always told me where he thought I should be and still he did not interfere with my journey. We were so close that, at our job, we would meet in the bathroom where there was a sitting room, to study the Word of God and pray. We would call off work and then meet at the park early in the morning and pray and this may sound crazy, but doves would fly over us while we were praying!

    It was him standing by my side in my first marriage when I came home, and my wife had taken everything, and I mean everything (except my baby grand piano.) He walked in and I was sitting on the floor, crying, and he never put her down, just said to me, "man you'll be alright. God has a plan and purpose for you." There are times when you think that someone is your friend just because he lives nearby, but God even loves us to the point that He will put people in your life and in your neighborhood.

    This friend was ordained by God to be there at the most critical times in my life. When I tried to kill myself, it was this friend who took me to the hospital. This same friend is still my friend to this day. He has a very big church. He is still married to the same women for over 20 years and right now, if I called him, he would be there just like in the beginning.

Friend number Four is a friend I met in church. At the time I was writing a book and so was he. We've been friends ever since. This friend is one of those guys who will fight with you all night and then still call you in the morning. We were real good friends because we had so much in common. He loves music and so do I. We started a radio station together and we also had a music studio. When I was pastoring, he was right there with me, even though he made it very hard for me, because he was a Bible scholar in my book. Whenever I would preach, if I said something that didn't sound right, I would look at him and he would be looking up right as I was preaching. I knew that, after the service he would say "man, we need to talk about what you said this morning."

He was put in my life to keep me balanced and to be that kind of friend who never allowed me to be 'too spiritual.' He and I have cried many nights together trying to figure out this relationship thing. He had his problems in marriage as well, but he never left me, regardless of how wrong he may have thought I was. And I tell you, out of all my closest friends, he was the one who would fight with me. We had many fights and still do. Yet, he understands me, and this is what makes a true and good friend.

Words from a Friend

Now is the time for you to step up, and do what you have been doing in private. Do this NOW in public! You know how you be singing in the house but will not sing in public? Or, how you help so many people over the phone but will not go back to school to get your degree in order to help them on another level? You make everybody laugh in your family but refuse to take that stage on open night. You need no speech, you need no okay from others, all you need is okay from your lips. This is your time, and yes, it's your turn.

Yes, it is scary, and you may be a little nervous but its your time. Remember that you had to go through all that God had chosen for you and you went through it in order to share this anointing and wisdom with God's people for the journey in their lives. I know that you think they will not hear you, or they might reject you, and I say so what? It would not be the first time. Why quit on the right side when you did not give up on the wrong side? You were chosen for this. You were being prepared before the old move died, before the church went bad, before your family broke up, before the children were gone - you were being prepared. Trust the teaching and your Teacher, because they are both still with you. You have the revelation for this hour. In your falls in life lay the hidden power for the next generations. So, take the falls, take them into the next level of God, the next level of love, the next level of worship and see what you saw in yourself.

I was that person who could help the world but would not even help or believe in myself. I could see your problem and then tell you how to get out but didn't believe in the same spiritual medicine for me. I have counselled so many married couples that are still married today, but I have been married many times and am still having trouble. If it was not for my real friends, who kept telling me, "it's not over because you've been married before," then I would have given up by now.

Positive words from real friends, sometimes, will take you back to *the real Word* from God. In the Bible, Jesus says to His disciples that he no longer calls them 'servant' but now calls them 'friend,' which means that I can now say some things to you that are personal, and you will not be offended later, right? It means that, when I tell you the truth about yourself, you will not say that I hate you but know that I love you.

Things to Remember When You Are Going Through

When you were a caterpillar you needed the ground, but now that you are a butterfly you need the air. Don't miss transition because you refuse to elevate your mind. Don't allow people to have you hating yourself because they don't see what you see or have what God has given you. There was a time in my life that I regretted the revelation that was given to me, because people would say, "where you got that from?" or "there you go being so deep." So, I started lying when I would speak and would say that another person said this, so that they would receive it as long as it didn't come from me. But God had to deliver me *from* the opinion of people in order to deliver me *to* the people.

Gravity was your help as a caterpillar, but as a butterfly gravity could be an enemy. Some of the same people who helped you coming up will hate you when you're passing them by. A good friend of mine told me once, that everybody who hears you will not follow you. I was getting upset when I would go and preach at places and people would say, "Doc, when you open up your church I will be the first member to join." When I finally opened up a church, none of those same people were there.

One lady, in my journey, was tithing to me when I had Bible study in my very little apartment (but never showed up for one of them) and the minute I got a building, she stopped tithing. Some people are in your life for a reason, others for a season and then there are some for a lifetime. Sometimes, only in extremity, do we discover what to live by. Understanding of this place is essential to our purpose and the reason why we are not dead. This is where life really is.

They say if it does not kill you then it will make you stronger. This place is in your mind and this place must be valued and protected at all times and at all costs. This is the garden to your destiny. No snakes are allowed: put up the signs and keep the alarm on in your heart. This is where dominion begins. It is only in this place, where you can be fruitful, multiply, and replenish the earth. This is the ground for you to become the tree for your life. This place will speak to you, bless you, and help you to become the *real you.*

But remember that every day you must die to self in order to stay in your rightful place. Remember that true rest is in you. The slave mind cannot destroy this place, but he can cause you to move and abandon this place forever. Without this place, you cannot be fruitful and multiply. Your true responsibility is to keep the glory of God in this place as your garment in the spirit. I just cannot say it enough that how we see ourselves is *everything.* Please, when you are looking at yourself - look through the eyes of the Lord. Looking by any other means could bring death, and this is a word from a friend.

There are Three Requirements for a Fulfilling Life

1. **A clear sense of personal identity.**
   Your identity cannot come from man but must come from GOD. You must hear God say, "you are my child" from your spirit. Without true identity, many other things will shape you away from your God given design.
2. **A deep sense of life's meaning**.
   Everyone must answer the questions: why we are here and also, what is the purpose of life? How does this thing called living, work?

3. **A strong sense of purpose and mission.**
When I think of purpose, I think of the original intent of a thing in the mind of the owner. Mission is the operation of the purpose as well. Purpose, mission, and vision are partners in life and all three must be understood.

How Do I See Myself?

No man can climb beyond the limitations of his own belief. Most of the time, the power of a thing not working is not because it lacks potential but because our minds have put limitations on it. You will always limit yourself if you need people's approval before you spread your wings. I remember a time when I was young, and I was playing my drums while a friend of my cousin, who also played drums, was watching. I began to tell him about playing doubles with my feet on the bass drums and he said, "no need to do that. It can't be done. No one's feet can go that fast." Because I trusted him and. at that time, he was a better drummer, I stopped trying. Until about a year later. I went to a concert and, low and behold, there was a man sitting on the drums playing doubles with his feet! I felt so hurt that I had let someone talk me out of what I believed I could do and what I had heard in my spirit.

Things like this have happened to me in so many areas of my life but, the truth is, that I allowed people to put limitations on me because I didn't understand my potential. When man puts a limit on what he can be, he has put a limit on what he *will* be. Understanding the importance of life begins with a realization of its great value, because you are here for a very great reason.

The Power from Within

There is a power within you and which must be activated then used, and always acknowledged. You have been given authority to be *the best you* every day of your life. The power that God has given you can lift your life to its highest level. This power can change illness into health, bring peace while removing turmoil, bring success out of failure, and victory out of defeat. This power can also bring companionship and happiness out of loneliness. Best of it all is that God's power will respond to you. **Remember that laws and principles govern life.**

Needed Things in Life - Universal Teaching Points

One of the greatest weapons for self-development is studying everything in life, from birth to death. The Bible says "for the invisible things of Him from the creation of the world are clearly seen; being understood by the things that are made, even His eternal power and Godhead; so that they are without excuse" (paraphrased). If you are trying to grow something, whether it be relationships or a business, always study the natural growth design of things.

Truth creates and confirms awareness. There is a truth that is given by God that will bring you into your created side, and this side of you is really where your blessing is. This side of you will show how to *see* what you saw in your spirit and in your mind. It is where your greatest ideas come from. It will also confirm that you are not crazy, that you have not lost your mind.

Strategies are made up of actions and tactics that convert visions to results for those determined to make things happen. The plans that are in you will amaze you. This is what I call the how-to principles that are living in us. One of the most important things in all that we do is to know the difference between positive attitudes and positive actions and, the flaw of counting one without the other.

Affirmation

This is one of the greatest enemies that I have had to face in life, because I believed most of my life that I was not affirmed, and because of this disillusion, I told my soul just to be. Regardless of truth, that creates and confirms awareness, great strategies and even a positive attitude with true affirmation from The Father Himself, you will still be lost if you choose to *do* nothing.

How to Get There

In order to get through, there are things we must *do* to get to the place where we belong. First of all, you can't quit, and you can't give up on hope. You can't say, "it's too late!" Pushing is a great part of the journey. Preparation is a very vital point as well. And you must know where you are going or if not, 'any old road' may get you there.

The Dreamer

You are going through the door...it's a new world on the other side, designed for you. This is why you're so uncomfortable where you are right now. Dreams come to those who are asleep. We must wake up and take responsibility of the dreams and bring them into reality.

The skill required for you to successfully live life is the 'power of imagination.' Without imagination, you will be bound by your present situation and probably die in your current dilemma. However, if you learn to dream you will free yourself from the time and place of your present circumstance and live in your original destiny, unmarred by time and sin.

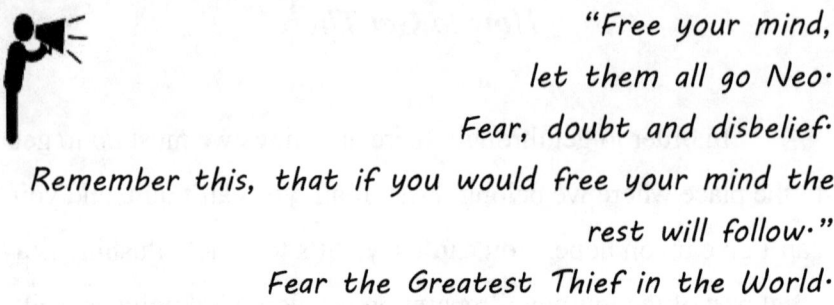

*"Free your mind,
let them all go Neo.
Fear, doubt and disbelief.
Remember this, that if you would free your mind the
rest will follow."
Fear the Greatest Thief in the World.*

I've learned that when you don't fight the spirit of fear, you will testify from the prison of criticism, jealousy, insecurity. Fear will be your human response. You would be surprised of all the things that fear has placed in my mind. I could be at the gym and a good-looking guy walks by. He would be very muscular and, because of my fears, I would say in my mind, "I hope my wife never sees him," or "is he the one that my wife will leave me for?" It is amazing how much we live under this spirit of fear. It overcomes us and to overcome it, we need to trust and love God completely.

    The Bible says that only perfected love casts out all fear. Well, if your love is not perfected then you are dealing with fear as well. *"There is no fear in love, but perfect love drives out fear, because fear has to do with punishment or loss and sometimes the truth about us comes from the place that we are hiding in."*

Called and Lost

What do you do when you are called, confused, gifted, and crazy? You can hear God and the devil. Yes, this was me and the first thing I learned was that you embrace these realities in your life. Learn to accept your humanity as well as your divinity. Also remember that you are not alone, for all of us are crazy (though we may not admit it!) When you look at the lives of any great man or woman in the Bible or outside of the Word you will see these things.

Peter, in the Bible, is a great example of how we struggle from within. Let's look at:

Luke 5:1-3a

[1.] And it came to pass, that, as the people pressed upon Him to hear the word of God, He stood by the lake of Gennesaret,

[2.] And saw two ships standing by the lake: but the fishermen were gone out of them, and were washing their nets.

[3a.] And He entered into one of the ships, which was Simon's, and prayed him that he would thrust out a little from the land,

Most of the time, when you see the Word referring to 'Peter' as 'Simon', I believe that he is thinking from his human side. And I say this because, most of the time, in the same text when his spiritual side is awakening, it now refers to him as 'Peter' or 'Simon Peter'. Let's read on and we will see this even here in:

Luke 5: 3b-11

3b. And He sat down, and taught the people out of the ship.

4. Now when He had left speaking, He said unto Simon, Launch out into the deep, and let down your nets for a drought.

5. And Simon answering said unto Him, Master, we have toiled all the night, and have taken nothing: nevertheless at Thy word I will let down the net.

6. And when they had this done, they enclosed a great multitude of fishes: and their net brake.

7. And they beckoned unto their partners, which were in the other ship, that they should come and help them. And they came, and filled both the ships, so that they began to sink.

⁸· When Simon Peter saw it, he fell down at Jesus' knees, saying, depart from me; for I am a sinful man, O Lord.
⁹· For he was astonished, and all that were with him, at the drought of the fishes which they had taken:
¹⁰· And so was also James, and John, the sons of Zebedee, which were partners with Simon. And Jesus said unto Simon, Fear not; from henceforth thou shall catch men.
¹¹· And when they had brought their ships to land, they forsook all, and followed Him.

These are the things that we go through when going back and forth from humanity to divinity. If you are not careful, it will drive you crazy or put much guilt on you. We see, also in the text that Peter only let down one net and not many nets, as he was told to by Jesus. This was because the human side thought Peter knew fishing and do you see that it took sinking to wake up his spiritual side? This is how God works a lot of times to bring us to the place where we are honest, with both sides of who we are.

I have made so many mistakes from the choices I made from my human side, thinking that "I know this," or "I can handle that one on my own." Immediately, when I began to sink, I wanted to be 'spiritual' and see it from God's side. Many times, I would be crying after I had sex in a hotel room. With the Bible in my hand, saying "Lord forgive me." But it was always *after* we had sex. This is us in so many ways, if we are honest.

We are called and confused until we learn how to hear our humanity but follow our divinity.

Regardless of the spiritual call on your life, your humanity will feel the price that you must pay to be obedient.
Luke 22:39-42

39. And he came out, and went, as he was wont, to the Mount of Olives; and his disciples also followed him.
40. And when he was at the place, he said unto them, pray that ye enter not into temptation.
41. And he was withdrawn from them about a stone's cast, and kneeled down, and prayed,
42. Saying, Father, if thou be willing, remove this cup from me: nevertheless not my will, but thine, be done.

Even Jesus understood the pain in the flesh and the limited amount humanity wants to suffer. He said, "Lord if you be willing let this cup pass from me." He knew that the drinking of this cup was a part of the purpose in which He was called, but at the same time, He was honest about His humanity.

If you really want to think that you are going crazy, try to lie about your humanity and where you are. This will take you over to the other side because God doesn't want us to deny our humanity. He wants us to surrender it, turn it over to God - not hide your humanity or act like you don't have it.

Jesus was in so much pain that an angel came unto Him from Heaven, strengthening Him. He needed help to deal with His humanity. Then the Bible says, "He being in agony, prayed more earnestly. His sweat was as if it were great drops of blood falling down to the ground." Being in prayer did not take away the pain of His flesh. It is through prayer and meditation on truth, that our strength is renewed to handle the pain of the flesh. Real talk is that your flesh will express how much life *the call* is talking out of you.

If it were not for angels and the grace of God, this will cause you to lose your mind. Your call will put you in lion's dens and fiery furnaces; it will have you walking on water and then almost drowning right in front of people and God. It has you being ship wrecked and telling people that it's going to rain when it has never rained before. Your call has you saying that you are having a baby but not by a man. Many people will think that you are stark mad, but you are not alone.

Wholeness is Your Heritage

My understanding of wholeness and my heritage in Christ Jesus is what really broke me *into* freedom. The right understanding was necessary to bringing me out of my false perception. People kept telling me to find who I was, and, if I were complete in God, then I would not have so many expectations from others. The weight that I would carry when they did not love me or respond to me in the way I thought I needed, would cause me to lose myself in pain, shame, and guilt. I started, again, wanting to die and became very depressed.

One day at work, talking to God, He said to me,

"Robert you were made for Me, and only in Me and in My purpose can you be fulfilled."

Then I had to ask myself, do I really want His heritage, or do I love being a victim? Because being a victim can make people feel sorry for me or care in a way I perceived as love.

When I say 'wholeness,' I am not talking about the ability to function, but the knowing of being complete alone. Many people are healed but not whole. When I think about the women in the Bible who had an issue in her body that caused her to bleed for 12 long years, could you imagine losing life for 12 years? Yet, when she came to Jesus and touched Him, she was healed! Her bleeding stopped. But then Jesus said to her, "your faith has made you whole." Her wholeness was in her mind about feeling like a woman again, getting her femininity back. Be content in *all* things but continue your search for wholeness. Sometimes, it takes asking God about your issue that makes you aware of not being whole.

First Be and Then Profess to Be

These lessons here may kill you, but this death is necessary because to be and know who you are sometimes goes against everything you may have been taught. See, *to be* means no need from the outside to exist; *just be*.
- Don't look for love, be loved.
- Don't look for happiness - know you are happy (i.e. be happy).

The believer must have a frequent God-presence from the eternal relationship, on a daily basis. As believers, we must prepare to know God better and love Him more. We must understand that God has always wanted to be with and in us.

First to Be Lit, and Then To Shine

This means to be content without doing anything. When Jesus was being baptized, The Father said publicly,

"This is my beloved son in whom I am well pleased."

The Father was not pleased by what Jesus had done but pleased because of *who* He is.

You must assume your rights to be you, because you were born an original. So don't die a copy. This will bring death to what you've become, and this may be very hard because you may think that you love *you*. It also may take many failures to wake you up to this place because success in a man owns eyes is his greatest delusion. You have the right to be you, which is really the only right that works for you. Staying you will become a task, at first, but the more you remind yourself of who *you are,* the more it becomes natural again.

Being you will begin to, also, bring fulfillment and it will help you release all that is inside. Once you are at this place, it will release *your place in life* and *rekindle your purpose*. Being you puts *you* back on the right train, meeting the right people. Staying in your original place will teach you that it's not what you do in public but how you think of yourself, in private, that really matters.

Your private times will be joyful and not bring thoughts of death like in times past. Being in the original place teaches us to speak from *whom* we are, not from *where* we are. This place is so beautiful, a place of contentment. One that you never will be removed from, regardless of where you may be. You will know who you are. You will be able to be in a place without making judgment or living with someone else's stress. This place shows you that anything other than you is a false standard of expression.

We must never allow life and its circumstances to frustrate our purpose. We must remember to watch as well as pray, for our purpose is too important to this earth and the nation to be aborted by negative mindsets and false standards. Regardless of how anointed you are and how much you pray; you are not immune to the appetite of the flesh. The flesh wants to eat anything that clouds your mind and leads you into a perception other than the truth of God.

Here is a word:

Proverbs 4:14-15

[14] Enter not into the path of the wicked, and go not in the way of evil,

[15] avoid it, pass not by it, turn from it, and pass way from it.

CHAPTER 34

Nevertheless, Not My Will

One of the greatest lessons for me was to be convinced that life *was not* about me. Regardless of my pain and my perception, God's will must prevail. I have seen the greatest people give up and make this thing of life about them because of their circumstances. I wanted to die because of how I was hurting but, even near death, I learned to be like Jesus. Yes, it hurts, and this pain is real in my reality, but I am not here for me.

God's purpose and will must be fulfilled in my flesh nevertheless. This attitude took growth and a lot of falling, crying, and complaining but the lessons were learned. I reflect on when Jesus was in the garden and the bitter cup before Him. This was the most trying time of His life, mixed with so many other things: Judas was about to betray Him and the Apostles can't stay awake with Him in the garden. He is sweating blood and The Father has presented the bitter cup for Him to drink. But in all of this Jesus understood the importance of the mission. He came here to redeem man and not to save Himself.

The most important thing to know about your life is that it's not yours. Many people may say, "then why do we have a will?" God gave us a will to use as free moral agents to express our love for Him and to be willing to do His will by choice, not force. We were created for His pleasure, not our pain. This is why where there is a crisis in love. There is also a crisis in the will to live. When you really understand this, then you will not use your will for your own gain or pleasure.

CHAPTER 35

Freedom by Death or Freedom by Truth and Life

My whole life I wanted to be free, but my freedom was not in asking for more knowledge of God, because that was my burden. It was the knowledge of God that brought me much grief. I believe that I was hated because of what God had shown me. By receiving much revelation, it brought conviction to others and rejection to me. So, I wanted out, and death was my plan. I thought freedom was in death; to die was to be released from all my battles. I would envision people killing me, or dying early and having people say, "he died in the Lord, yes." I was sad and depressed, because the rejection that I was giving God and the lies that I wanted to believe were like gravity to my soul. We can never be free if we lie by night and tell the truth by day. You are where your thoughts are.

My mother was a smoker and the doctors told her that smoking was killing her and especially because she had very poor circulation. And then, on top of that, she smoked. She would rather suffer in her comfort than suffer for her deliverance. So, I was told that, right before she died, she was given an oxygen tank to help her breathe. She had said that she did not want no tank and that she will not stop smoking. My mother took off the tank, lit her a smoke and died. This same demon had visited my mother and gave her a mindset that freedom by death was her only way out. This was not the truth, and as hard as it was for me to lose my mother that way, it helped me to say,

"No, I will not quit regardless of my marriages; my much disappointment. And yes, I will fight for purpose and love and truth. I have declared freedom by life in Christ and not freedom by death!"

You Were Assigned to Break the Curse
(Bringing the Curse to The Cure)

The curse was brought to you, so that you would put it on the cross and free all that comes out of you from this curse. You were trusted with trouble, by God, to stop trouble from ruining your life and that of your family. One of my sons in the ministry called me and said to me, "dad, I was doing a revival and having a prayer line when a young lady came up to me and she was pregnant. With tears in her eyes, she asked to me why would God do this to her? She went on to say that she didn't want the baby." My son in the ministry thought this was a young lady who was ashamed or who hated her boyfriend or maybe just the fear of having a baby. Still, when he asked her why she said that, she said "because my brother, who just got out the line with joy in his heart that God loves him and has forgiven him, was the one that raped me and now I am pregnant with my brother's baby."

He asked me "what can I tell her?" I said, "tell her that rape and immorality was in her family, but God will raise her and the child. This trouble was given to her to break the curse off the family and the curse is broken with her because she brought the curse *to The Cure*." These kinds of things and circumstances are hard to embrace but we all must accept our assignments.

You were assigned to break the curse, by first being *you* and accepting the call along with the pain. Yes, it is easy to right them and then go through it. I find that I have to do both, and you may have to also.

The First Curse is Not Being You

How wrong is it for you not to be you? Do you know that the first suicide was when Adam ate from the Tree of Knowledge of Good and Evil? This caused him to hide from God, (which was really running from himself). For most of our lives, we are trying to be someone else; trying to please family, friends, husband, wife. But who are you?

When I think about the story of the prodigal son, I ask myself, "was he lost because he left home or was he lost to himself?" Because, when he came to himself that's when he went home. Home is where love and The Father are, and we can never come home unless we find ourselves, because that's where love and The Father lives.

This is the attitude that I had to take. No more blame, It's okay for me to *be me,* to like my smile, my walk, and my freedom *to be me.* Right now, and that's all that I have - I will be me. At an appointed time, just like a baby who cannot be hidden anymore, the God in you will get rid of all jealousy because you will never again want to be anyone else.

Be You

I've been in music all of my life, and it's funny how we try to do things just to please others, sometimes at the expense of ourselves. Having confidence in what God designed you to be is necessary in fulfilling your purpose. There were times I would try to play drums like the other drummers or make music like other musicians. Not knowing that I was really willing to kill my image and my expression. Instead of playing the way God gave it to me, I would change it or just not reveal it rather than take the risk of being rejected. Then, later in life, I would hear someone else doing the same things that I was thinking about doing but because of fear my expression had become lost. Now they are famous, and I am still at the house, being someone else.

This taught me a thing or two, about being the person you are - which can be hard when you have a need to be accepted and a need to be loved. You would rather do what they like and be who they want you to be, just for their acceptance, instead of being yourself and dealing with being rejected. I have learned that it takes power to remain you in a storm of rejection. The fear of being lonely will have you playing roles that can kill the very core of who you are.

The Bible says to love your neighbor as you love yourself, which means that loving yourself is *key* to relationship. You may be afraid but, one day, you must make up your mind and just do it, just like you do when no one is around. The way you heard it, the way you saw it and stop crying about doing it your way, especially if it's not the way God gave it to you. God has placed everything in you that is required to be the person He called you to be.

An apple seed has everything in it to produce the tree that produces the apple. Everything was placed in the seed by God. So, the question should be if your identity developed or not? Do you really know who you are, and are you happy being you? How long can you remain true to yourself and can you remain true to yourself in the midst of others that may not look or act like you? How much do you believe in your self-worth? Can you see the value that you carry? If you don't see your own worth, then why ask it from others?

When a house is up for sale, there is a thing called an appraisal, which is when a person comes and gives the value of the house, *to praise the house*. When was the last time you gave an appraisal to your own house, to see the value that God has place in you? And remember, just like a house's value goes down by the neighborhood that it is placed in, your value can also be appraised at a lower value by the thoughts that live in your 'neighborhood' of your mind. There is a pretense that we are inadequate, on our own, to build, but this is anything other than the truth. Unless we have truth about ourselves, anything else would be out of place. We must have a revelation of our place. Who we are, as a person, and the purpose of all that God has put into us.

Your spirit knows your destiny, but do you listen to your spirit rather than the words of others? You must begin developing self-confidence because this will give you the ability to handle a relationship with *you* as well as with others, without thinking that you are at the lowest of the totem pole.

The Curse is Broken When the Word was Spoken

Hebrews Chapter 11:3

3. **Through faith we understand that the worlds were framed by the word of God so that things, which are seen, were not made of things, which do appear.**

There will come a time in your life that you get tired of just settling with whatever comes along. I believe it is a sin to just sit back and allow life to pass you by. You have to begin to say, "there will be a difference in my life because I have been created to make a difference!" A lack of knowing self will always lead to a lack of knowing what you want. I have a question, "what are you doing with your *now*?" I know many things have come your way, but is it over? Did you decide to quit, for that's the only way you can lose. We know that's not the will of The Father for your life. You know it is so easy to give up rather than to fight. We have, for so long, just stayed in the race not to win but to say that we are in something. Stop that, and take the mind of God, be in it to win it!

    Be like Christ, while you are yet on your cross in life, say "it is finished." The truth of the matter is that there is too much power in your mouth to settle for whatever comes your way. Would you rather believe in luck or believe in faith? See, if you couldn't make a change and you were powerless and without resources, then this would be another story, but the truth is that there is nothing that can lock you down. There is no limit on what you can believe or think, so why settle?

    Right now, with the breath in my body, I breathe and speak. I have the right to laugh, the right to smile and the right to be me, right *now*. I have been given the right to frame my world with the Words of God. I speak what I want to see. I say what God has already said, and His Words are already established but are waiting to be activated *by what I say*.

    Visa can send you a pre-approved credit card, but the use of it would be unavailable until you call and activate what has already been pre-approved. God says, in His Word, that if you abide in Him and He abides in you then you can ask what you will. It also says when you pray say, "Thy kingdom come, Thy will be done on Earth as it is in Heaven." These are the Scriptures that reveal the pre-approved credit in Heaven by the spoken Word.

If God is my example and He started out by creating things out of what he said, this tells me two things: That the power to create is in God and in His Words and because I am made in His image and in His likeness and He has been given permission to use His Words, then I am also able to create my world - frame it and benefit from it by what's in my mouth. Now you may ask, "Robert what does that mean?" It means that I (Robert James Duvall Jenkins) right *now*, stop blaming anything and anyone. Nothing can curse me, because when I am true to myself, I break the curse. As long as I am free to be me, with no blaming, no excuses, no expectations, no entitlement from people, then the curse is broken when The Word was spoken.

Now, this has been a very challenging time for me, for God had begun to wake me up at many levels. First, I had to face my fears in order for my dreams to come true. I, also, had to learn how to finish my course and how to embrace the unknown pains and not trace them to the previous past that I had lived. It seems to be so easy for us to believe the negative. We will embrace doctrines on devils, hell and the fall of Adam but this same book also writes about God, love, peace, the place called Heaven and most of all, the power of words. I believe the greatest power in man is the spoken word, the invisible power of the unknown. Let's stop repeating the sin of our first father Adam, by using the blame game and let's win by repeating the words of our last father Adam by using the Word game. It is time for us to take responsibility and change what we see. Why complain when we can make a change? But you first must believe.

One of the many reasons why God's Word is so wonderful and powerful is because it is from eternity. Whenever you hear a Word from eternity remember that it will run out of time and continue to run until the Word becomes flesh - for the eternal Word never expires, only transform and transcend time. The only reason why you would see an eternal Word in time is because it has a date with time *and* you. Stop missing your dates and having your husband (God) waiting for you. Call Him up right now and say, "meet me at the place designed for us." Your faith and God's Word must agree to create the world in which you were designed to live in.

CHAPTER 36

The Power of Words

Whenever the enemy is talking to you, remember that you are talking to The Father of Lies and a thief. His job is to deceive you with words, and his reason is to rob you of God's glory. When we look at the story of Adam and Eve in the book of Genesis, it was not that they saw their nakedness for the lack of clothes, but they saw their nakedness from losing the covering of God's glory. The devil knew that, when Eve started talking to him, her words and focus would begin to change.

Atmospheres can cause you to think from different levels and shift your thoughts to a place that is far from where you can hear God clearly. When you listen to your fears or your doubts, if you are not careful, your words will change as a result. It is just like a hotter temperature can make you feel sleepy. The devil's deception was placed on making Eve think that God did not have her best interest in mind and that He was holding something from her.

Remember that there is more truth hidden in a lie than is revealed in the truth. If I lie about what's in a dark room and you click on the light, you can see what I was lying about. However, you don't know why or what caused me to lie. The real power in a word is, sometimes, what was *not* heard.

Remember That Jesus Said Me and My Words are One

By the spoken word of God, I have become the "ever living," because He, who is eternal, lives in me. Because God has a plan then there must be a journey, and we, as the people of God, should not stop until we reach the place for which we were created to occupy by our words.

The Words You Speak

The words you speak will do four things with regards to your personal life:

1. Your words locate you;

   Your words reveal what is inside of you, what's in your heart. If you listen to what you have been saying, then you will know where you are.

2. They will reveal whether you are in fear or faith, forgiveness or un-forgiveness, belief or unbelief;

   If you listen to others when they speak, this will help you to locate them as well. This is a major principle in counseling.

Matthew 12:33

³³· Either make the tree good, and his fruit good; or else make the tree corrupt, and his fruit corrupt: for the tree is known by his fruit.

James 3:2

²· We all make many mistakes. If anyone does not make a mistake with his tongue by saying the wrong things, he is a perfect man. It shows he is able to make his body do what he wants it to do.

> 3. Your words fix the landmarks of your life.
> The words you spoke yesterday make your life what it is today. Jesus said that you could have what you say. You are today what you said you would be yesterday. (James 3:2-5)
>
> 4. Your words affect your spirit.

James 1:26

²⁶· If a person thinks he is religious, but does not keep his tongue from speaking bad things, he is fooling himself. His religion is worth nothing.

> You have two sets of ears—an outer ear and an inner ear.

Whatever seeds you sow in your heart—your heart will produce that fruit.

Mark 4:9

9. And he said unto them, He that hath ears to hear, let him hear

Mark 4:23

23. If any man have ears to hear, let him hear.

The Effect of Words

Proverbs 13:2-3

2. A man shall eat well by the fruit of his mouth: but the soul of the transgressors shall eat violence.
3. He that keeps his mouth keeps his life: but he that opened wide his lips shall have destruction.

Proverbs 15:4

4. A wholesome tongue is a tree of life: but perverseness therein is a breach in the spirit.

Proverbs 18:20

20. A man's belly shall be satisfied with the fruit of his mouth; and with the increase of his lips shall he be filled.

Words in the Home

The atmosphere of your home is the product of words.

Proverbs 16:21-24

21. The wise in heart shall be called prudent: and the sweetness of the lips increaseth learning.

22. Understanding is a wellspring of life unto him that hath it: but the instruction of fools is folly.

23. The heart of the wise teacheth his mouth, and addeth learning to his lips.

24. Pleasant words are as an honeycomb, sweet to the soul, and health to the bones.

    Use your words to encourage others and to build healthy and positive self-images. Learn to make your words work for you, not against you!

    To curse simply means, "to call evil upon," "to speak against," or "to speak negatively of." A Christian can be cursed by speaking negatively about someone or something.

Mark 11:12-23

12. And on the morrow, when they were come from Bethany, he was hungry:

13. And seeing a fig tree afar off having leaves, he came, if haply he might find anything thereon: and when he came to it, he found nothing but leaves; for the time of figs was not yet.

14. And Jesus answered and said unto it, No man eat fruit of thee hereafter forever. And his disciples heard it.

15. And they come to Jerusalem: and Jesus went into the temple, and began to cast out them that sold and bought in the temple, and overthrew the tables of the moneychangers, and the seats of them that sold doves;

16. And would not suffer that any man should carry any vessel through the temple.

17. And he taught, saying unto them, Is it not written, My house shall be called of all nations the house of prayer? but ye have made it a den of thieves.

18. And the scribes and chief priests heard it, and sought how they might destroy him: for they feared him, because all the people was astonished at his doctrine.

¹⁹· And when even was come, he went out of the city.

²⁰· And in the morning, as they passed by, they saw the fig tree dried up from the roots.

²¹· And Peter calling to remembrance saith unto him, Master, behold, the fig tree which thou cursedst is withered away.

²²· And Jesus answering saith unto them, Have faith in God.

²³· For verily I say unto you, That whosoever shall say unto this mountain, Be thou removed, and be thou cast into the sea; and shall not doubt in his heart, but shall believe that those things which he saith shall come to pass; he shall have whatsoever he saith.

    Very often (too often) Christians curse their homes, their lives, their families, the businesses, etc., without realizing what they are doing. Complaining about tough times and how bad things are is an open doorway for Satan to deliver tragedy to your home.

James 3:5-12

5. Even so the tongue is a little member, and boasteth great things. Behold, how great a matter a little fire kindleth!

6. And the tongue is a fire, a world of iniquity: so is the tongue among our members, that it defileth the whole body, and setteth on fire the course of nature; and it is set on fire of hell.

7. For every kind of beasts, and of birds, and of serpents, and of things in the sea, is tamed, and hath been tamed of mankind:

8. But the tongue can no man tame; it is an unruly evil, full of deadly poison.

9. Therewith bless we God, even the Father; and therewith curse we men, which are made after the similitude of God.

10. Out of the same mouth proceedeth blessing and cursing. My brethren, these things ought not so to be.

¹¹· Doth a fountain send forth at the same place sweet water and bitter?

¹²· Can the fig tree, my brethren, bear olive berries? either a vine, figs? so can no fountain both yield salt water and fresh.

Carnal Christians find it easy to speak with a worldly tongue. It is easy to think and speak negatively because the world is geared and programmed this way. An unscripted confession is a confession of death, defeat, and failure. It is a proclamation of the supremacy of Satan. Such confessions only glorify the work of Satan in your life. They will destroy your faith and keep you in bondage. With your mouth (not with your heart) you will determine who has control of your life, God or Satan.

Faith Must Speak

There is no such thing as faith without confession.
Mark 11:22-24

²²· And Jesus answering saith unto them, Have faith in God.

23. For verily I say unto you, That whosoever shall say unto this mountain, Be thou removed, and be thou cast into the sea; and shall not doubt in his heart, but shall believe that those things which he saith shall come to pass; he shall have whatsoever he saith.

24. Therefore I say unto you, What things soever ye desire, when ye pray, believe that ye receive them, and ye shall have them.

Romans 10:8-10

8. But what saith it? The word is nigh thee, even in thy mouth, and in thy heart: that is, the word of faith, which we preach;

9. That if thou shalt confess with thy mouth the Lord Jesus, and shalt believe in thine heart that God hath raised him from the dead, thou shalt be saved.

10. For with the heart man believeth unto righteousness; and with the mouth confession is made unto salvation.

Start confessing your faith over your fears.

2 Corinthians 4:13

¹³· We having the same spirit of faith, according as it is written, I believed, and therefore have I spoken; we also believe, and therefore speak;

>Examine each thought: if it is not of God, throw it away. Proclaim God's word instead.

2 Corinthians 10:4-5

⁴· (For the weapons of our warfare are not carnal, but mighty through God to the pulling down of strong holds;) ⁵· Casting down imaginations, and every high thing that exalteth itself against the knowledge of God, and bringing into captivity every thought to the obedience of Christ;

>Soon, you will have far fewer doubts and fears. Speak the answer, not just the problem. Your confession will liberate you *or* imprison you. The rules for liberation have not changed just because you made the confession of Christ as Lord and Savior. To *confess* Christ is so different from *living* like Christ.

Thoughts come from one of two sources:
1. Our flesh.
2. Our spirit.

Satan uses the appetites of our flesh as food for him. God speaks to us through our spirit.

Romans 8:5-7

5. For they that are after the flesh do mind the things of the flesh; but they that are after the Spirit the things of the Spirit.

6. For to be carnally minded is death; but to be spiritually minded is life and peace.

7. Because the carnal mind is enmity against God: for it is not subject to the law of God, neither indeed can be.

What's in Your Mouth?

What I am about to say will probably blow your mind but, believe it or not, you are only in the situation that you are in because of two things: One, what you have said out of your mouth; and Two, what you did *not* say out of your mouth. Remember this: words are the controller of the ship. If you don't like where you're going, change what you're thinking and what you're speaking. Also remember that your thinking and speaking *must* agree.

Mysteries to The Spoken Word

God saw the light and that it was good. Remember God *saw* what He *said* **before** He called it *what it was*. Now, this is a very deep mystery. Why didn't God just say, "let there be day?" Why was it necessary to say, "let there be light" and then *call* the light 'day?' Here is the divine order:

1. Say *it*.
2. See it *be*.
3. And then call it *what it is*.

Too many times we want to call it *what* it is before we see it *be* what it is. In other words, we want it to be in the following order:

1. Say *it*.
2. Call it *what it is*.
3. See it *be*.

God divided the light from the darkness, which is another mystery to the Bible (Genesis 1). Is it possible for light and darkness to be in the same room together? Is it possible for you to have unity with both? Darkness is the symbol of the undeveloped, so what God is demonstrating is when we begin to speak, we separate the undeveloped from the manifestation. Light is only in darkness *until* you speak. From that moment, the power of the spoken word will begin to reveal what was spoken, *not created*, but what was released.

Let's look at this again: God divided the light from the darkness. The question is, was it divided because He spoke light into existence or was it because, without His call, they would have remained as one? God called the light 'day,' and darkness He called 'night'; and 'the evening,' and 'the morning' was the first day.

Another mystery is the evening and the morning was the first day *not* the morning and the evening. Question: why was the evening referenced first? Could it be because He called the light out of the darkness and from the moment light began to appear (evening), the *day* had begun?

The power of the three principles

There are three points which I would like to talk about:
1. The God *said* principle
2. The God *saw* principle
3. The God *called* principle

The God said principle is the principle of the spoken word, and we must believe its power. Let's look at how God brings everything into existence because of what He says.

For everything we read in Genesis Chapter 1 comes from the God said principle. This is foundational truth - that all things started from the spoken word. There is a scripture in the Bible that says the power of life and death is in the tongue. It does not say that life and death are *in* the tongue, but that the *power* of life and death is in the tongue. It's not just what you say, but it is the authority given to what you say which makes what was spoken so powerful.

A person could walk up to me and say, "you are under arrest." If this person is not a police officer and has not been given the authority by law, then he cannot arrest me. Even though these words are real to him, he cannot, legally enforce them because he has not been given the authority to. God has put the greatest responsibility on man when He gave him the authority to speak life or death.

The God saw principle is the principle of vision or perception. This came to me when reading Genesis 1:4 that God saw the light. This speaks to me in volumes because, many times, what we see is *not* what we said. When our vision is blurred we may not see what we said. The God saw principle must be in line with what we said. God said, "let there be light" and then He saw that the light was good. The enemy will always fight us on our visions or perceptions. Most of the time, we have a crisis between what we said (believed) and what we have seen come to pass. We love to say, "as it is in Heaven, let it be on Earth," but have you *seen* what's in Heaven in your life? The saw principle is the *evidence* of the spoken word. It's also hope coming alive. This principle is also what Eve used to eat the forbidden fruit in her mind. The Bible says in Genesis 3:6 that she *saw* the tree was good for food and pleasant to the eyes, and a tree to make one wise. Here we see the saw principle at work against her and God, because it had the power to take her to a place, whether good or bad. Remember, when you say you saw something, you are referring to the past, which means it has already happened. God first used this principle, but the devil caused Eve to use it to disobey God. God saw that the light was good, but Eve saw that the forbidden fruit was good for food and pleasant to the eyes.

Many times, in my life, I have used this principle in a forbidden way and it has hurt me very much in my journey. This principle is also what it means to look upon a woman with lust in your heart. The Bible says when you do this, that you have sinned already because you *saw* it in your mind's eye. The past means it was *already* done. This is a very powerful principle and we must not use it without the leading from the Holy Ghost. There are many things that we have seen that were not presented by God. These things must die in the seeing stage before we called them into our truth. It is time for us to take responsibility and change what we see if it is not in alignment with what God sees for our life.

When we look at the God saw principle we see it at every phase of man. Let's look at Genesis 6:5. God *saw* the wickedness of man: every imagination of the thoughts of his heart was only evil, continually. It made God repent that He had made man on the earth. This principle is what God used to see the wickedness of man and because of what He saw, it caused God to be the first person to repent.

The God called principle is connected to the God said and God saw principles as well. All three of these principles are in Genesis 1:3-5. The God said principle is the spoken word principle; the God saw is the vision and perception; and the God called principle is the label of the God said principle. The God said principle is from the *mouth*; the God saw principle is from the *eyes*; and the God called is also from the *mouth* but *by the mind*. All three of these principles are found throughout the Bible.

God uses these three principles in the beginning of all things but so does the devil. When it comes to life, we must ask these questions: what did they *say* to me? What are they *seeing* in me? And what do they *call* me? Whether good or bad, these questions make a great impact on our lives.

The God called principle is so important because it <u>seals</u> all three. Many of us have been called things that did *not* reflect what God said or saw. When we accept the name-calling of others and begin to be a slave to what we were called, this is a bad thing. These three must always agree. What I am being called, and what God saw and said must work *together* to bring God glory. This is the foundation of my design. When I accept anything besides what God has said, seen and called, I am now being reshaped.

The great part about all three of these principles is that we have access, with the guidance of the Holy Spirit, to use them. I believe the greatest power in man is the spoken word, the invisible power of the unknown. The Bible tell us, in Romans 4:17, "As it is written, I have made thee a father of many nations, before him whom he believed, *even* God, who quickened the dead, and called those things which be not as though they were." God uses this principle all throughout the Bible as well. These principles are a part of our inheritance. The choice of words you speak are *so* important to your journey in life. Many things shouldn't be, but they have power because we called them into place. The words you speak will do three things with regard to your personal life:

1. Remember, your words locate you.
2. They reveal what is inside of you and also what's in your heart; and
3. They will reveal whether you are in fear or faith; forgiveness or un-forgiveness; belief or unbelief.

Luke 6:45

45. **A good man out of the good treasure of his heart bring forth that which is good; and an evil man out of the evil treasure of his heart bring forth that which is evil: for of the abundance of the heart his mouth speak.**

Jesus said that you can have what you say:

Mark 11:33

³³· The power of these three principles has everything to do with what has shaped our lives. What have you called that God did not called for you?

Call for Change
Change Happens One Step at a Time

It's our time to stop processing things that are not in line with the will of the Lord. This comes from a made-up mind and knowing what we believe in and what God has said to us. Jesus would say, "according to your faith let it be unto you." We must call for this change. Make a demand on the will of God for your life.

One of the greatest places in your life is when you are clear about the will of God concerning your 'it.' Knowing His will gives me confidence in speaking what He has already declared. The greatest thing that the devil can do to you is influence you to close your mouth. We must know that the devil is counting on *your perception* of so-called failure to use as ammunition against you.

Do not accept failure as failure! The first principle is to understand that change is a process, not an event. Therefore, change requires time, energy, and the resources to support it as it unfolds.

Never Close Your Mouth When God Has Put a Word in It

One of my greatest gifts, which is also my greatest battle, is my gift to talk. When you have a place in life, you must know that your place comes with warfare. All lands are fought over, either to protect or conquer. Your land is where your gift lives and most of the time it is your *mouth*.

Even the Apostle Paul said this, about Israel, that the word was in their mouth. This is the same gift that my grandfather had as well, and he was hated because he'd stand up for the truth and not be silent. Great leaders such as Malcolm X and Martin Luther King were also known for specking their minds. The word that is in your mouth is worth the suffering, persecution, and many other things, even death. But God has trusted you with it as it is His Word that you carry. Never allow anyone to lock His Word in by closing your mouth and not releasing it to the world.

Paul was in prison and they had him locked down but at midnight, which is the darkest hour of the night and the enemies start of activity, he opened his mouth and an earthquake caused him to be set free. How many people would still be in chains if we, who were given The Word in our mouth, would speak? The Word that is in your mouth, is *needed* in the world.

CHAPTER 37

Victories

Victory is yours! God has no intention of allowing you to lose the battles of life. How can man lose at life when life is your gift from God? This victory is something that God gives us. We don't have to earn it. Like salvation, victory is a free gift of God's grace.

When we are in this fight, let's always remember that it is a fixed fight! Jesus paid it *all* with His blood, and His blood has not been shed in vain. Our fights' victory is like a prepaid visa card - you've already been pre-approved! Just get in the ring to activate it. We praise, in advance, that we've won, because of the cross and the blood of Jesus. Victory to us is credit given by God. So, all our debt, bills, troubles and fights - charge it and then leave with the goods.

Romans 8:37

37. No, in all these things we are more than conquerors through him who loved us.

Exodus 9:16

16. And in very deed for this cause have I raised thee up, for to shew in thee my power; and that my name may be declared throughout all the earth.

Just Like God's Name is Declared
So is Our Victory

There are many times in boxing that it looks like one of the boxers have lost the fight. You cannot go by what he looks like or how many times he's been hit. The judge can still declare him as the winner, because they are counting the hits from both contestants. If the truth be told, we have been hit by the devil many times and we're still standing. It is because we are not fighting this fight by ourselves. Remember, there is someone *else* in the ring of life with us.

We are victorious, not because we are always winning, but because *the Judge of Life granted our birth and revealed our destinies*. He said, and has declared, we are victorious! We do not walk in the ring *trying* to be a winner, *we come in as the winner*.

Ephesians 6:14a

14. Stand therefore, having your loins girt about with truth,

We are the heavyweight champions and we have the belt of truth to prove it. We have the title.

Romans 8:37

37 Nay, in all these things we are more than conquerors through him that loved us.

We were born and trained to win! Just like Moses, we were trained by the enemy, so that none of his tricks would work. The first word in the Bible is the word '*In*' and the last word in the Bible is '*Amen.*' The reason why we are victorious is because *God is*:

In a-men = IN A MAN

THE ENEMY CANNOT BEAT GOD.

AND GOD IS IN ME.

GOD IS IN A MAN FROM THE BEGINNING TO THE END.

CHAPTER 38

The Law of Faith is The Law of Release

We find, in the Bible in Genesis 1, every day God releases something into that day. He says, "let there be" and there was. The Word 'let' means 'to release something.' By this, God is our example of how to surround our world by our words. You are here to distinguish the thoughts of the present day from that of a previous generation, and to grow every day in your words. Selah!

According to your faith be it unto you.
Mark 11:23

23. For verily I say unto you, That whosoever shall say unto this mountain, Be thou removed, and be thou cast into the sea; and shall not doubt in his heart, but shall believe that those things which he saith shall come to pass; he shall have whatsoever he saith.

The power of the Word is hidden in our belief, but the enemy of our words is - fear. Sometimes, our fear makes us say something is "too good to be true" or that "it's too simple for us to just believe." We have been taught that if it's too good to be true then it may not be. Well then, that would end grace, mercy, and having the mind of Christ.

Faith

The first law of release is that every law contains, in itself, the principle of its own expansion. It will set us free from the limitations which that law, at first, *appeared* to impose upon us. You can never look at an apple seed and know how many apples can come out of it. This is also true in every spiritual law of God. The limitation was never in 'The Law,' but in the conditions under which it was working. Our power of selection and decision enables us to provide new conditions, not of your own accord, but that provided by nature.

The specialization of each Law discloses enormous powers which have always been latent in it, but which would forever remain hidden unless brought to light by the co-operation of faith and the opening up of our mouth. This is a Personal Factor. The Law itself never changes, but we can use it by realizing the principle involved and providing the conditions thus indicated. This is our place in the order of the universe. We give definite direction to the action of The Law, and in this way our Personal Factor is always acting upon it. This happens whether we are aware of it or not. The Law, under the influence thus impressed upon it, is, all the time, re-acting to us. Faith is a law in the sense that electricity has laws, just as there are also laws of aerodynamics.

There are laws working in the body as well. If you operate within the laws of electricity or aerodynamics, you are safe, they perform well and are dependable. However, if you break those laws, they can kill you. Likewise, if you operate within the law of faith, it too, will be safe, perform for you, and will be something to depend on. Just like when Peter was walking on the water, really he was walking on the word '*come*,' with his eyes focused on Jesus. Yet, when he took his eyes off of Jesus, and heard the storm and saw the wind, he began to drown.

Be aware of the thoughts of the enemy; remember in:

Ephesians 4:14

14. That we henceforth be no more children, tossed to and fro, and carried about with every wind of doctrine, by the sleight of men, and cunning craftiness, whereby they lie in wait to deceive;) see faith in the word could allow him to walk but fear allow him to fall.

Romans 12:3

3. For I say, through the grace given unto me, to every man that is among you, not to think of himself more highly than he ought to think; but to think soberly,

according as God hath dealt to every man the measure of faith.

Man is a creature of faith. That is to say that he was created to live *by faith*. Man is driven by something in him to place his faith, (like an anchor), in something or someone - in the desire to feel safe, sound, and whole.

The Power of Faith

When I see the power of the Word it makes me think of authority and keys. Remember in the Bible when God told Peter that He had given him the keys to the kingdom? Peter is the symbol of faith, so this reveals to us that when we are awakened to the true identity of Christ, we will begin to have access to the principles of the Kingdom that bring the manifestation of God on Earth.

Whenever you are given authority, you are also given the right to make decisions, to change laws, and to establish rules. One of the root words for authority is the word 'author.' An author is the person who writes the book or the thoughts behind the book, or is the originator of the writings. When I think of keys, I think of access and the ability to unlock *and* lock doors. These thoughts alone should make you think before you speak.

CHAPTER 38

The Law of Faith is The Law of Release

We find, in the Bible in Genesis 1, every day God releases something into that day. He says, "let there be" and there was. The Word 'let' means 'to release something.' By this, God is our example of how to surround our world by our words. You are here to distinguish the thoughts of the present day from that of a previous generation, and to grow every day in your words. Selah!

According to your faith be it unto you.
Mark 11:23

23. For verily I say unto you, That whosoever shall say unto this mountain, Be thou removed, and be thou cast into the sea; and shall not doubt in his heart, but shall believe that those things which he saith shall come to pass; he shall have whatsoever he saith.

The power of the Word is hidden in our belief, but the enemy of our words is - fear. Sometimes, our fear makes us say something is "too good to be true" or that "it's too simple for us to just believe." We have been taught that if it's too good to be true then it may not be. Well then, that would end grace, mercy, and having the mind of Christ.

Faith

The first law of release is that every law contains, in itself, the principle of its own expansion. It will set us free from the limitations which that law, at first, *appeared* to impose upon us. You can never look at an apple seed and know how many apples can come out of it. This is also true in every spiritual law of God. The limitation was never in 'The Law,' but in the conditions under which it was working. Our power of selection and decision enables us to provide new conditions, not of your own accord, but that provided by nature.

The specialization of each Law discloses enormous powers which have always been latent in it, but which would forever remain hidden unless brought to light by the co-operation of faith and the opening up of our mouth. This is a Personal Factor. The Law itself never changes, but we can use it by realizing the principle involved and providing the conditions thus indicated. This is our place in the order of the universe. We give definite direction to the action of The Law, and in this way our Personal Factor is always acting upon it. This happens whether we are aware of it or not. The Law, under the influence thus impressed upon it, is, all the time, re-acting to us. Faith is a law in the sense

Whatsoever a man thinks, so is he. If he becomes, by just thinking, then how powerful is the agreement of thinking and speaking? Think about it. Faith is so powerful because it allows us into the unseen realm. When we read the Scriptures in Genesis 1, they should cause us to see how powerful the invisible realm is. Also, how everything that is tangible and visible really comes from the invisible realm. This also brings me to the point in Genesis Chapter 1 where it talks about how God said, "let there be light." When I read the Bible, I ask myself a lot of questions especially in the book of Genesis Chapter 1, for in our origin are the foundations for all truths.

God said, "let there be light." This statement should cause us to think about "if God is light and He is everywhere then why would He say let "there be light in the place where He was?" Could this have been the first time that light was created? If so, was God always light for we know that He has always been."

The truth to me is not that this was the first time that light was created but how God is teaching us that everything comes from the eternal. Also, that it is our job to release these words and cause them to be manifest in our lives. So, why does the Word of God say let there be light? Remember, the word *'let'* indicates the releasing of something. Whether you believe this or not, everything that you need is already in your mouth. We just need to learn how to release it and then frame it, by faith, and the words we speak afterwards.

If we know, that in our mouth we have the power to change anything that we want and the power to produce great results from nothing, this should also tell us that we ought to talk about the things that we want to see live and grow. Remember that thoughts are the previews of the 'coming attraction' and words are the movie that sync us to God's movement. I have come to learn that God's thoughts are words, but God's words are pictures. This is what I call the 'three in one principle'.

1. Thoughts, the beginning of all things;
2. Words, the address to all thoughts; and
3. Pictures, the image or the mind or the vision behind all thoughts.

These three are the complete circle of all creation and, in the spirit, you can see these in all things.

In the natural, pictures are the physical images of invisible thoughts which can be drawn, painted or taken by a camera. In the book of Genesis we have the voice of God (which are God's thoughts) and in the book of Exodus, which is the second book of the Bible, we have Moses (his name means 'to draw out'. In other words, all of God's thought must be drawn out). Moses was drawn out of the water (water is a symbol of the Word as in Ephesians 5:26). Then, after Moses, we have Joshua (whose name means 'savior' and is also the same name for Jesus), who is the picture of the very image we should manifest on Earth.

Think about a camera that has a built-in light and an eye *(I, me)*. The Bible says when the eye is single it is full of light. The devil told Eve that "the day you eat of this tree your <u>eyes</u> shall be opened." The whole purpose of the system of the enemy is to *blind* you *while* he *steals* the spoken word concerning you and your life. You may say, "how can the devil steal the spoken word concerning my life?" Easy! By getting you to do *for his system* the thing that you have not done *for God's system* and speaking what *he* has planted. He's planted doubts, fears and disbelief, mistrust, and then deceives you into *speaking* the things that he has planted. By the power of your words, you bring these things into your reality. This is why we must hear the Word of God, and this is how the eternal Word crosses over to time.

We speak from *whom* we are, not from *where* we are in the natural. If, from the beginning of time, God created the Heavens and the Earth and I am His son, then, in all of my being I should create the atmosphere of my physical world by my words - just as God. One of the most important lessons that God taught me was that most problems start in a crisis of faith. One of the main questions that is asked of me, in many situations, is "what do we do when we are paralyzed in the face of odds?" My response has been to "speak to yourself, use your words to build yourself up."

Remember what David did in one of the most critical times of his life? He encouraged himself! Many times, things have not changed because we try to repair *things* before we repair *ourselves*. Don't learn the power of your words and then not use their power to repair you first.

CHAPTER 39

God's Purpose and Our Problems

We must know the difference between God's purpose and our problems, never allowing our problems to stop us from doing His purpose. Still, at the same time, never ignoring our problems because of God's purpose in our lives. Holiness is still a character of God. It's amazing how everybody wants God's love, but rejects His character and holiness. We all know that a gift comes without repentance, but we need offer more repentance than the gifts received.

What God has called us to do and the gift(s) that have been given to us, is ahead of our time. It's from eternity and because of this, we must bring our character to a place of maturity. If not, our gifts will take us to a place that our character can't keep us and the class (journey) starts all over again. Without great character along with a great gift, your lack of character will only bring destruction to God's name, and all that you stand for. I believe this is the reason why God allowed Joseph to be put in the pit and the prison because his gifts were given to him at such a young age, but his character still needed to be developed.

We must understand the need for balance. It is a very heavy burden to know that the things you hear and see from your gift may be the first time that they are released in the earth realm. This is also one of the main reasons why you must remain true to yourself at all times and at all costs. Remember you have a problem because you have a purpose, but without knowing your purpose, your problems will win and keep caging you in.

All false perceptions come from lies that we live by when accepted, which seemingly seem to be successfully rooted in our minds. Without knowing your true purpose, false perceptions will be a problem never faced. It's good when the wrong things no longer work. This is a not a problem but it's purpose waking up and taking over our will.

In closing

I hope that these teachings and expressions of my life will unlock you from your false perceptions, launching you into your divine destiny. It has taken me many years to be honest and, with the strength from God, to put down my selfish ways.

My heart is for all people to be free to serve God and have no false perception of Him or themselves. The more you hide and lie the longer truth will wait to set you free. But why wait any longer? Consider being free today!

PLEASE LEAVE A REVIEW, MUCH APPRECIATED!

ABOUT THE AUTHOR

Apostle Robert Jenkins lives with his wife, Cassandra, in New Orleans, Louisiana. They are the founders of Divine Insight Ministries and the Apostle is one of the trustees of the ministry, In My Father's House.

Divine Insight Ministries is a multicultural, Bible-based, Spirit-filled ministry, that engages in reaching the hearts of mankind, by first introducing their hearts to God.

Apostle Robert Jenkins has many years of Bible training and has traveled throughout various parts of the world during his 40 years of preaching. He has a revolutionary ministry gift and is known for revelatory preaching. He continues to share a God-inspired word, which is in high demand by both by clergy and laity alike.

The command of God on Apostle Jenkins' life is 'the awakening of oneself to truth.' His endeavor, for God's people, is that:

- Purpose is revealed;

- Passions are renewed; and

- Principles are restored.

"I believe that the key to every believer is knowing that the truth comes from within. God bless."

Apostle R. J. Jenkins